TWICE CHOSEN

TWICE CHOSEN

Charles Hoffman
A Convert from Judaism to Roman Catholocism

Queenship

Queenship Publishing Company
P.O. Box 42028
Santa Barbara, CA 93140-2028
(800) 647-9882 FAX: (805) 569-3274

Publisher's Note

In order to reduce the cost of this book, the author has requested to not receive any royalties.

©1995 Queenship Publishing

Library of Congress Number 95-68114

ISBN: 1-882972-56-2

Published by:
Queenship Publishing
P.O. Box 42028
Santa Barbara, CA 93140-2028
(800) 647-9882 FAX: (805) 569-3274

Printed in the United States America

Declaration of the Author

The references contained in this book regarding the current apparitions in Medjugorje, is presented with the knowledge that the final judgment thereon rests with the Holy See of Rome, to whom the Author and Publisher willingly submit.

Dedication

I dedicate this book to Mary, the Mother of God. No other person can better lead us to know Her Son Jesus, as well as direct us towards holiness, than Our Blessed Mother.

Contents

Acknowledgments

I express gratitude to my wife Sara, who typed this manuscript and provided encouragement, patience, and understanding. Without her prodding this book would not have been written.

The editing and proofreading of this book by Elly Andree, a member of my prayer group, is greatly appreciated.

Most Reverend Michael D. Pfeifer, O.M.I
Bishop of San Angelo, Texas

FOREWORD

TWICE CHOSEN describes the wonderful faith journey of the author, Charles Hoffman, as guided and directed by our loving God, Who is Father of Abraham and of Jesus Christ. He sums up this journey in Chapter Four, where he states, "God never takes back His gifts or revokes His choice. Therefore Israel remains the chosen people and this call has not been revoked but continues. I will be eternally grateful to God for being 'twice chosen'; first, to begin my life as part of the Old Israel and, secondly, to end my life as part of the New Israel."

This journey began with the belief in the one God, and terminates with the acceptance of the central mystery of Christianity which is the Blessed Trinity. At the end of this inspirational book, the author, who is faithful to Abraham and to Christ, proclaims "Hear, O Israel, the Lord our God, the Lord is one: Father, Son, and Holy Spirit."

TWICE CHOSEN portrays in a vivid way how the author has also been touched by God through many human agents in his life parents, spouses, children, relatives and friends, but especially by the One Who is the greatest of all humans, Mary, the mother of Jesus and our mother. This most beautiful of all women has touched Charlie's life in a most intimate way as his mother and sister in faith. The author's devotion to Mary is summed up in his own words, "During my life as a Jew, Mary meant nothing to me. Only when I realized that Jesus was my God, did I know then that Mary was also my mother. And I thank Jesus for sharing His mother with me. By honoring Mary, I honor Jesus her Son."

In **TWICE CHOSEN,** the author not only shares his faith-story, but brings much clarity and insights to many basic teachings of the Jewish and Catholic faiths. All who read this book will surely come to a new appreciation of the God of Israel, Who is also the God Jesus, and of all those who believe in Him. May this faith journey the author inspire many other sons and daughters of Abraham come to accept the One Who is the true Messiah - Jesus Christ.

PREFACE

On February 23, 1992, I celebrated the twenty-ninth anniversary of my baptism and entry into the Roman Catholic Church. At this point I had spent half my life as a Jew and half as a Catholic. Some times the question is asked, "If a Jew becomes a Catholic, does he still remain a Jew?" For me the answer is quite simple. If being a Jew means living the Mosaic way of life, the answer is no. But a follower of Moses, who becomes a Catholic continues in his love of Moses and adherence to many of his teachings, plus the spiritual guidance of Jesus. While the convert from Judaism to the Church is no longer a Jew in the religious sense of the term, he continues, as a Catholic, in his love of the faith of his fathers of old in Israel, seeing in Catholic principles and practices Judaism full-blossomed.

I will always be thankful to God for the joyous years I spent as a Jew and for allowing me to know and practice the faith of ancient Israel. It was a great preparatory experience for me and eventually led me to recognize Jesus as the Lord and Messiah of Israel. Those early years as a Jew have helped me live a more meaningful life as a Catholic.

Many people can recall at least one great conversion experience in their lives. God has blessed me with two of them. In the first one, the Holy Spirit led me to know that Jesus Christ was my Lord and Savior and the Catholic Church which He founded was the new Israel. In the second experience, Mary, the Mother of God, led me to Catholic orthodoxy after having spent many years a Catholic liberal. The first conversion process took about two years, the second only three months. The Holy Spirit led me to know Jesus and His Church intellectually. Our Blessed Mother led me to know Her Son on a more personal basis.

For several years my wife Sara has been encouraging me to write about my conversion to Catholicism. I pray that this book can be an instrument of the Holy Spirit by helping those of the Jewish faith, who are searching, find their Messiah Jesus; and those Catholics or other Christians, who are either searching or confused, to see the real beauty of the Catholic Church as the fulfillment of the promises God made to Israel.

Orthodox Judaism goes back to the time of Abraham. Historically, the term Orthodoxy distinguishes the more inflexible type of

Judaism from its less conservative counterparts within the Jewish tradition (Conservative and Reform Judaism). When referring to Judaism in this text I am speaking of Orthodox Judaism. In the religion of Jewry today, Orthodox Judaism is closest to "Ancient Judaism."

— Charles Hoffman, 1994

CHAPTER 1
THE JEWISH YEARS

YEARS IN GERMANY

In 1933, Adolph Hitler rose to power in Germany. This date marked the beginning of the end for millions of German Jews, as well as others, who lived in countries occupied by the Nazis. By the end of World War II the Nazis had murdered six million Jews.

In 1925, my father Abraham Buchanek, then sixteen years old, left Poland for Germany. He changed his name to Hoffman, reasoning that with a German name he would succeed. There, in 1931, he met my mother Selma and married her the following year. I was born in Berlin on October 10, 1933. My mother who was German by birth became a Polish citizen the day she married my father. I too became a Polish citizen at birth. At that time in Germany wives and children possessed the same citizenship as their husbands and fathers, respectively. It was our Polish citizenship which eventually saved our lives. At my circumcision, eight days after birth, I received the names Karl, Karol.

Unexpectedly in 1938 my mother and I had an opportunity to leave Germany. Concerned for my father, she made him leave instead. She thought Nazis would not harm Jewish women and children. She had no idea about the horror soon to unfold. My father left Germany and went to Cuba.

Memories of my early years in Germany are dim except for one night etched clearly in my mind. The date was November 9, 1938 — a night of terror for German Jews. I will never forget "crystal night," even though I was barely five years old. Jews were brutalized and killed, their synagogues and businesses destroyed. That night I was staying with my aunt and uncle in their apartment. The building itself surrounded a square interior courtyard. At one side of the complex stood a synagogue. Suddenly a group of Nazi youths and men ran screaming into the yard and headed for the synagogue. They broke every window and pew, then threw the sacred scrolls (Torahs) into the courtyard and burned them. From our vantage point, we were very frightened. We kept the lights out in the apartment hoping the mob would not notice us. Many acts of terror were repeated that night as crystal (glass) rained on the city.

After 1938, it became extremely difficult for any Jew to leave Germany. Yet somehow my mother and I managed to leave in May 1939. Only the Lord knows why we were so fortunate. If we had not gotten out then, we would have been killed in one of the concentration camps (probably Auschwitz since we were Polish citizens) along with some of my Jewish relatives. With one thousand other Jews my mother and I left on a ship called the "St. Louis," bound for Cuba. Upon arrival, the Cuban government would not grant us entry. After a week of futile discussions, our ship left Cuba and headed for the United States hoping for asylum. The U.S. Congress debated our fate and then refused us entry. Unfortunately our German captain had no choice and headed the ship back to Europe. He did not want to return to Germany because he knew only too well what would happen to us. Finally, after intense negotiations with several European countries, England, France and Holland accepted us. My mother and I, including three hundred other Polish citizens, fortunately went to England. The seven hundred Jews holding German citizenship were accepted by France and Holland. Eventually they died in concentration camps when Nazi troops occupied those countries. In the 1970s, Hollywood depicted our journey in a movie called "Voyage of the Damned."

YEARS IN ENGLAND

From 1939 to 1943 my mother and I lived in London, England. Originally my parents had owned a tailoring business in Germany. In London my mother found work as a seamstress. In September 1939 Great Britain declared war on Germany. By 1941 the German air force was bombing London almost every night. Almost every night during 1941 to 1943 was spent in air raid shelters as the city came under attack. Again, I was to have an experience I would never forget. One night the air raid sirens did not go off in time to warn us although we could hear the German planes overhead and bombs falling. All of a sudden there was a big explosion. My mother grabbed me out of bed and ran outside the house. The next morning we returned to assess the damage. My bed was completely covered and buried under walls and bricks. If my mother had not pulled me out of bed, I would have been killed. The explosion, caused by a bomb called a block-buster, had landed only two houses away. This type of bomb could demolish five or six houses at once. By God's grace it

2

missed the house by ten feet, landing instead in the back yard. If it had struck the house all of us would have been killed instantly. Once again God saved my life.

In 1940, when I was eight years old, I began my education in the Orthodox Jewish faith. A Hasidic rabbi instructed me privately until my mother and I left England in 1943.

COMING TO THE UNITED STATES

My mother and I arrived in the United States in May 1943 settling in Brooklyn, NY. Already living in New York City were my grandmother and my mother's three sisters who also had escaped from Germany. My father came to America from Cuba in 1941. In 1943, he joined the U.S. Army and was stationed in the Midwest. During this period my parents separated and soon after divorced. I saw my father once after the war ended in 1945, and then, not again until 1962. He never kept in touch with me, although I knew he remarried and had a daughter. It was my mother who raised me alone without support for either of us from my father. One of the first things my mother tried to do after our arrival in America was to enroll me in a Yeshiva. Yeshiva is the orthodox Jewish equivalent to a Catholic school. Barely ten years old, I had set my ambition on being a rabbi. But the Yeshiva cost money, much more than my mother could afford. As an independent private school without support from a central institution, the Yeshiva had no way to subsidize the poor. Therefore, I went to public school and received my religious instruction at the local orthodox synagogue I attended. Although my mother made sure I received a good education in the Orthodox Jewish faith, and that I practiced my faith, she had little religious training herself. Until I turned thirteen, she insisted upon my attendance at all Sabbath and Holy Day liturgical worship services. In Judaism, the Sabbath is holier than any of the Jewish Holy days.

We lived in a predominantly Jewish neighborhood, where I attended a public school. Ninety percent of the students were Jewish. Most of my Jewish friends were Reform Jews who never went to Sabbath worship services at the synagogue. Instead, they would be playing in the school yard every Saturday morning while I went off to worship. Admittedly, there were times when I wanted to be with my friends and skip the synagogue. But my mother kept close watch over me, making certain I obeyed her. As I grew older, I was grateful to her for being strict. On November 2,1946, I made my Bar Mitzvah. Where circumcision symbolizes a male's entrance into the Jewish community, Bar Mitzvah is his rite of initiation into Jewish religious responsibility. While Bar Mitzvah is not specifically mentioned in the Bible, allusions to the rite from Tradition suggest the practice dates back to very ancient times. The first definite reference to Bar Mitzvah dates from the thirteenth century. Theory postulates that a father bears the sin of his son until the son is thirteen years old. Thereafter, the boy is personally responsible for his actions. The father, accordingly, recites the following prayer: **"Blessed be You our God, King of the Universe, Who has relieved me from punishment for this one (the son)."** The implication was not that the father abdicated further care for his son, but that from that moment the boy assumed greater responsibility for his actions. If Bar Mitzvah frees the father from certain duties, it also means the son assumes new obligations covering the gamut of Jewish faith and practice. I remember vividly my Bar Mitzvah in 1946 as one of the greatest days in my life. I had just turned thirteen. It meant that I was now a "man." I could be counted as one of the ten men required to participate in certain parts of the synagogue liturgy. The tremendous spiritual high I experienced extended into my daily life. I even started going to daily morning and evening liturgical services at the synagogue. If I couldn't go to the synagogue, I would pray the liturgy parts allowed at home.

At the age of fourteen I decided to become an aeronautical engineer. I entered Brooklyn Technical High School in 1948 and graduated in 1952. Students at Brooklyn Tech came from all parts of New York City. Ninety-eight percent professed the Christian faith. During those years some of my closest friends were Christians. In 1951, at the age of seventeen, I joined the New York National Guard because I wanted to attend the Military Academy at West Point. I felt this was the only way to get there. I never made it to West Point because foul-ups prevented me from taking the entrance exam. In 1953, before starting college, I volunteered for four-months active duty and attended the Infantry Leaders' School at Ft. Benning, GA. After missing out on West Point, I entered Polytechnic Institute of Brooklyn in 1953, majored in electrical engineering, and graduated with a BEE degree in 1957.

In 1956, I met and married my first wife Irma Rosenbaum. Although also Jewish, she knew almost nothing about her religion because Her parents were basically agnostic. They never went to synagogue nor did they observe the Jewish festivals. In 1957, our first child was born. Eight days after his birth he was circumcised and given the name Stephen.

CHAPTER 2
JUDAISM AND ITS BELIEFS

It is my mother to whom I owe a great debt because she made sure I received a good Jewish education and, more importantly, that I practiced my faith. This religious foundation eventually led me to Christ and the Catholic Church.

Many Christians and, sadly, many Reform Jews have little knowledge of Judaism. Jews themselves dispute who exactly is a Jew. Etymologically, the word is easily defined. The name comes from Judah, one of the twelve tribes of Israel. Later it came to be applied to anyone belonging to the Hebrew race, and finally to those who profess the Jewish religion. The unresolved question is whether Judaism is mainly ethnic or religious, since there are many Jews who are not direct descendants of Abraham, and many others who may be so descended but do not profess the Jewish faith. Perhaps the best explanation defines Judaism as the heart and Jewry as the body of a permanent moral tradition whose roots date back to the prophets of Israel and whose hopes lie in a forthcoming Messianic era. Both root and hope are deeply religious and very distinctive. Too many people prefer to think of Judaism as the parent of Christianity and Islam — and no more. They forget that Judaism is a living faith whose vital elements have remained substantially unchanged and yet, paradoxically, the Jewish people have greatly changed over the centuries. Before relating the process of my conversion, it would be helpful to look at the sources from which the Jewish culture derived and to summarize some of the key Judaic beliefs. Many of these beliefs are similar to those I hold as a Catholic.

THE BIBLE

Any discussion of Jewish belief must begin with the Bible. Hebrews call it Tanakh, from the initial letters of the words Torah, Neviim and Ketuvim. The Torah, also known as the Pentateuch (Greek word for five: pente) contains the first five books of the Jewish and Christian Scriptures. The Torah is also referred to as the Law. The Neviim represents the books of the Prophets. Hagiographa

(Ketuvim: writings) covers the third part of Jewish Scripture — those books not in the Pentateuch or Prophets.

The five books of the Pentateuch (whose Hebrew names are taken from the first significant word in each book) are Genesis, Exodus, Leviticus, Numbers and Deuteronomy. Genesis tells the story of creation, of man's history until the time of Abraham — father of the Jews — and the tales of the patriarchs. Exodus describes the departure from Egypt, still symbolic of Jewish migrations; giving of the Law (Torah) to Moses on Mount Sinai, and construction of the Tabernacle to house the Ark of the Covenant with its tables of the Law. Leviticus, formerly known as Torat Kohanim (the priestly code), contains legislation given to Moses after the Tabernacle was built and covers mainly the laws of sacrifice and impurity together with moral and social directives not found in Exodus. Numbers recounts the wandering of the Israelites in the desert and gives additional legislation. Deuteronomy, also known as Mishnah Torah (Repetition of the Law), recapitulates the laws of Sinai, with variations, and records the last sermons of Moses.

Since the First Temple played such an important role in Jewish history, the prophetic books are divided on this basis. The Former Prophets relate Israel's history from the conquest of Canaan to the destruction of the First Temple (586 B.C.) as covered in the following books: Joshua narrates the conquest and division of Canaan; Judges continues the Biblical story until past the time of Samson, who exemplifies the Jewish desire for freedom; Samuel gives the biography of Samuel the prophet and the first two kings of Israel, Saul and David; and Kings spans the period from the reign of Solomon to the destruction of the Temple in Jerusalem by Nebuchadnezzar. The Latter Prophets of major importance include Isaiah, Jeremiah and Ezekiel. Isaiah appears as the seer of eternal peace at the end of days when the Lord's Anointed will judge the nations. Jeremiah remains as a constant reminder to the Jews to keep the covenant their forefathers had made with God. Ezekiel, the great prophet of Jewish Messianism, promises through Israel a final establishment of the rule of peace in the world. The twelve Minor Prophets are cited within a single book. According to rabbinic teaching, the prophetic spirit ceased with the last of the Minor Prophets. Since then, the role of teachers in Israel has been assumed by the men of the Great Synagogue and the wise men who succeeded them. They received the faculty of interpreting biblical prophecies. Indeed, according to the Talmud, "a Sage is higher than a Prophet," because without the sage a prophet might not be understood. Once the Messianic age appears, however, the ability to prophesy will return to Israel.

Hagiographa (Writings) is a collection of twelve books, or eleven if Ezra and Nehemiah are treated as a single work. The Psalms comprise a collection of prayers and hymns, many taken from the ancient Temple service. Today they form a major part of Jewish liturgy. Proverbs gather together numerous parables and statements of wise counsel. Their theme, mainly addressed to the young, and postulates a belief that due reward will ultimately come to the good (synonymous with the wise) and retribution to the wicked (identified with the foolish). Job is a religious dialogue concerned with the mystery of suffering and its relationship to sin. Five scrolls (megillot) follow the book of Job which are commonly read in most synagogues on special occasions. The idyllic story of Ruth, set in the period of the Judges, is recited for Pentecost. The Canticle of Canticles includes a series of love poems used at Passover. Lamentations prayed on the day of fast (ninth of Av) recall the tragedy that befell the Temple and Jerusalem under the Babylonians and commemorate the destruction of the First and Second Temples. Ecclesiastes reserved for the Feast of Tabernacles meditates on the passing nature of human life on earth. The Esther story of persecution under Persian King Ahasuerus is read annually at Purim. Finally, the Hagiographa contain the Daniel narrative from the Babylonian Exile and the prophet's apocalyptic visions; Ezra-Nehemiah spans events after the return of the Jews from Babylon; and Chronicles, now in two parts, summarizes the history of Israel until the end of the Babylonian exile with special attention to the kingdom of Judah.

A distinction should be made here between the Bible of the Jews and the Old Testament of Christianity. Seven books of the Old Testament, as received by Roman Catholics and the Eastern Orthodox faith, are considered Apocrypha by the Jews. While some Jewish scholars believe there were originally two independent canons of the Hebrew Bible, others defend their original unity citing the intimate relationship between various pre- Christian Jewish communities. The two canons have come to be known as the Palestinian, used by Jews in and around Palestine, and the Alexandrian, accepted by Jews who were dispersed in other lands. The Alexandrian canon, available in the well-known Greek version of the Septuagint, was completed about 132 B.C. It differed from the Palestinian in the order of the biblical books and in its greater extent. The threefold grouping into the Law, Prophets, and Writings was absent, and several other books, not found in the Hebrew Bible of Palestine, were included. These include Wisdom, Ecclesiasticus, Judith, Tobit and Baruch, and in most manuscripts the first two books of Maccabees.

By the end of the first century A.D., the Pharisees of Palestine decided against the Alexandrian canon on the basis of four criteria. These are still invoked by Jewish authors in determining the revealed word of God: (1) the book in question had to conform to the Pentateuch, (2) it could not have been written after the time of Ezra, (3) it had to be written in Hebrew, and (4) it must have been written in Palestine. The following books were all expunged from the biblical canon: the book of Baruch and the epistle of Jeremiah, which were not of Palestinian origin; the books of Sirach (Ecclesiasticus) and First Maccabees written after the time of Ezra; Tobit and parts of Esther and Daniel, composed originally in Aramaic and also probably outside of Palestine; Judith, likely written in Aramaic; and Wisdom and Second Maccabees, originally penned in Greek. This canonization of the sacred scriptures was completed by the academy of the Sanhedrin, which met in Jabneh (Jamnia), a city of Palestine south of Jaffa. After the destruction of the Second Temple (70 A.D.), Rabbi Johann ben Zakkai reestablished the Sanhedrin at Jabneh until the Bar Kokba revolt (135 A.D.). At some unrecorded period between these two dates, the Hebrew Bible was formally determined.

When speaking of the Apocrypha, Jews reference the term carefully to noncanonical Jewish literature written during the period of the Second Temple and up to the Bar Kokba revolt. They freely admit that it contains works similar to those in the Bible and actually found in the Septuagint, but excluded from the canon for the reasons given. The Protestant reformers in the sixteenth century reverted to the Jewish canon of the Old Testament, using the same principles invoked by the Sanhedrin of Jabneh.

TALMUD

Along with revelation of the written Torah (first five books of the Bible) was a revelation of an Oral Torah (that is, interpretations of and deductions from the Scriptures) that accompanied the Scriptures themselves. Jews relied on the Oral Torah because no written text could serve as a complete guide of conduct; written text must have some form of oral commentary associated with it. From the fifth century B.C. onward there was a conscious effort on the part of teachers to expound on the canonical books of the Torah and to make their meaning and application clearer. A priest and reformer,

Ezra (frequently called the father of Judaism), appeared on the scene in 428 B.C. and reshaped Israel.

To the study of the Law of Yahweh (Torah), to practicing it and to teaching Israel its laws and customs. (Ezra 7:10)

Not only did Ezra establish the program Israel would follow, but the colleagues whom he attracted to himself — the Soferim, or "Scribes" as they were called — literally became the "Men of the Book." The Scribes took words implicit in the Book of the Torah of God and made them explicit and intelligible. Under their tutelage too, as required over time, they issued enactments and decrees.

And Ezra read from the Law of God (Torah), translating and giving the sense, so that the people understood what was read. (Nehemiah 8:8)

The scribes conducted their teaching and legislating orally through their schools and councils, in order to distinguish carefully between what was the Written Torah (Scripture), and the body of exegesis (interpretation by word of mouth) — the Oral Torah. The activity of the Scribes and the results they accomplished, became the heritage of later Jewish sages who continued to study, instruct and legislate along the same lines. These later sages, roughly from 200 B.C. to 200 A.D., became creators of what is called the Mishna. What were their intellectual and spiritual works?

They interpreted the Scriptures: a number of their interpretations indeed were acute commentary on the plain meaning of the Biblical text, its difficult and rare words, its legal injunctions and its homiletical intent. This exegetical activity is known as Midrash, i.e., the investigation and exploration of Scriptural content. By means of exegesis they strove to find Scriptural support for laws and regulations that were operative in their society. When conditions warranted, they created enactments or preventive measures. In the course of time, as these oral teachings and enactments accumulated, distinguished masters undertook to put the substance of the law into some systematic and logical form, in other words, into a Mishna.

If pre-Christian Judaism is unintelligible without the Bible, the Jewish faith since the Christian era is unexplainable without the Talmud, the main repository of Judaic tradition. As a collective name, Talmud means "instruction" and comprises two sets of writings: the third-century Mishnah, compiled by Rabbi Judah about 215 A.D., and the fourth to sixth centuries' Gemara, which has come down in two forms, the Babylonian written in Eastern Aramaic and the Palestinian in Western Aramaic.

From the early third century the Mishnah supplanted numerous earlier collections putting an end to much controversy between various rabbinical schools. The Mishnah, therefore, is not an original work but a redaction of earlier material written in the typical Hebrew style of Jewish scholars at that time. Each of the six divisions — Seeds (laws on agriculture), Festivals and Women (marriage laws), Injuries (civil and criminal regulations), Holy Things (worship and ritual), and Purifications — is divided into two parts or Tractates. These are further subdivided into chapters, and the chapters into paragraphs or precepts. As a sectarian law-code, the Mishnah builds on the principle of precedent, giving the sayings of learned Rabbis, in quotation or paraphrase, and often only a sentence in length. Most of the legislation is extremely minute. Indicative of the high regard in which the Talmudic tradition was held, a Mishnah in the treatise Sanhedrin decrees that "the punishment of him who transgresses the decision of the Scribes is more rigorous than for that which is plainly written in the Scriptures."

Gemara is the commentary on the Mishnah. Both Mishna and Gemara are now included in the Talmud with interpretation following rabbinic tradition. Jewish authorities in Babylonia organized those laws which had developed from the close of the Mishnah down to their own times; their commentaries together with the Mishnah received the name Babylonian Talmud. It represents the final codification of Jewish law. In Palestine the law was less organized, mostly because of unsettling conditions under the Roman Empire. What exists, however, bears the name of Jerusalem or Palestinian Talmud.

If the Mishnah appears detailed, the Gemara is minute in the extreme. The Talmud is difficult to understand because it is a code of laws, a case book, and a digest of discussions and disputes that went on among various rabbis. Interspersed are reflections of every kind, at times its contents as motley as a daily newspaper. Now and then the recorded opinions are dissimilar or even contradictory. It is not only the variety of opinions recorded in the Talmud and other rabbinical literature that hamper their appreciation, but also the style — brief, telegraphic, often bare to the bone — makes the Talmud inaccessible without a guide. The heads of the two leading rabbinic academies of Babylonia provided such guidance. From the sixth to the eleventh centuries their authority was supreme over all Babylonia

— which in the meantime had become the center of all Jewry — and, thus, for most of that time, their authority extended in other countries as well.

The Talmud makes no pretense of being a code or catechism listing Jewish obligations in categorical form. Rather, it records the process by which the Mosaic law is clarified. How important is the Talmud in Jewish life? The Talmudic sages had made up their minds that all Israel — not merely some small elite group — would study Halakah and live by it. Halakah is that part of the Talmud devoted to laws and ordinances not written in the scriptures but based on their oral interpretation. And that is why post-Talmudic rabbis made the Talmud the central source for Jewish study, thought, and practice, without any really serious dissent.

Protest movements arose against Talmudic authority in the sixteenth through eighteenth centuries. But for better or worse, the emphasis put on Halakah and halakic study by the Talmudic sages was permanent, so that all philosophers, novelists, poets and moralists had to acknowledge the sovereign role of the Talmud. Unless one were ready to become a schismatic he had to come to terms with Talmudic Halakah. Today, Orthodox Jews believe in both the written law (Scriptures) and the Talmud. For them, one cannot be valid without the other because there is no such thing as private interpretation.

CONCEPT OF GOD

The Talmudic conception of God is clear. Echoing the Torah, Jewish rabbis saw Yahweh as not only one God but uniquely as the eternal Almighty whose knowledge encompasses all things past, present, and future. He is infinitely greater than the created world He brought into being, and yet mysteriously dwelling in His creatures. Absolutely just and perfectly holy, He is merciful to those who invoke His name and benevolent to all mankind.

Idolatry in the Talmud and Midrash means a brazen denial of God's unity. For how can a man simultaneously worship another human being or an element of nature, and at the same time pay homage to the invisible God? Jews are encouraged to suffer martyrdom rather than participate in the prevalent idolatry around them. A possible tampering with the doctrine of God's oneness was the Christian belief in the Trinity. The Trinity was understood to mean Tritheism (i.e. three distinct gods).

Divine omnipotence and omnipresence were so forcefully described in the Bible that rabbinic scholarship was satisfied to repeat the scriptural passages or, more often, merely refer to the inspired text. But God's omniscience was a different matter. Conscious of the problems that would arise when seen in conjunction with human freedom, the Talmudists went out of their way to stress existence of both realities.

On the traditional side, we read that God's infinite knowledge cannot be doubted. A classic passage in the *Ethics of the Fathers* states without qualification that God knows everything, but leaves man with his own liberty intact:

> 'Everything is foreseen, yet freedom of choice is given; and the world is judged by grace, yet all is according to the amount of work.' The relation of God's decrees to man's freedom is not always plain. If there are ambiguous statements in classic Judaism about the reality of man's freedom in the face of omnipotence, the general outlook is never in doubt. God is sovereign but not one who undercuts human liberty. Quite the contrary, through the rightful exercise of freedom, as in prayer, man can literally 'influence' the Lord of Hosts: 'Just as the pitchfork turns over the grain from one place to another, so does the prayer of the righteous reverse the decisions of the Holy One, blessed be He, from the attribute of anger to the attribute of mercy.' (Ethics of the Eathers)

By the third century B.C., the name Yahweh was considered forbidden to human lips. Adonai (my Lord) took its place. Alexandrian Jewish translators who produced the Septuagint simply wrote "the Lord."

The theme of contemporary Orthodox prayer stresses awareness of God's majesty. He is Lord by the twofold title of having brought the universe into being and of surpassing, by the transcendence of divinity, all the works of his hands. No matter how deeply God's transcendence may have been emphasized, Judaism today would not be the same if the intensely personal God had been turned into a remote deity. The later rabbis, too, stressed that God was unlike man. At the same time they tried to express the warm relationship between God and Israel through concepts such as the Shekinah, His indwelling among creatures. The Shekinah was said to go with Israel into exile, to dwell among the people even in their uncleanness, and to weep at the sadness following Jerusalem's destruction. As used in the Talmud, and understood by Jews today, Shekinah may mean the presence of God in the Temple of old, particularly in the Holy of

Holies, or some earthly sign of the hidden celestial glory of Yahweh, or merely the radiance of God's infinite presence among men.

TORAH AS WISDOM AND LAW

Judaism was born of the belief that God, for all His transcendence, condescended to reveal Himself to His people. Through patriarchs and prophets, He spoke to the chosen race, and through them to the rest of mankind, telling them what to believe, Whom to worship, and how to conduct themselves in accordance with His will. It is an axiom of Jewish faith and typical of its orthodoxy that religion is no mere construct of human reason but an obligating gift of divine revelation.

As discussed earlier, Torah refers mainly to the first five books of the Bible and, by an extension of the word, to the whole Mosaic law. But its fundamental meaning for a Torah-true Israelite is "divine communication" which binds the receiver to believe and to act on what he believes God tells him to do.

As one reads through Talmudic literature, the first impression is that Torah was mainly concerned with commandments. But this is misleading. As perceptive as it is, the Torah is primarily instructive in wisdom from above. Yet its wisdom is not speculative but practical, and not so much reflective on truth as effective in producing goodness.

In the Talmud we find the following statement which refers to the Torah: "PRECIOUS IMPLEMENT WITH WHICH THE WORLD WAS CREATED." The following commentary from classical Jewish commentators (11th and 12th centuries A.D.) regards the above passage:

It is written, With the beginning God created the heaven and the earth (Genesis 1:1), and the word 'beginning' refers only to the Torah, as it is said, The Lord acquired me as the beginning of His way (Proverbs 8:22). It says also, Then I was by Him as the instrument of His craft (Proverbs 8:30): Says the Torah, 'I was the instrument made use of by the Holy One at the very beginning' — for God studied it and created the universe accordingly... Everything that was created, was created only for the purpose of fulfilling the Torah. All the things under the heavens, all of them, are only the means of satisfying the needs of those who devote themselves to the Torah.

Therefore, the man who reads and lives the Torah radiates the heavenly knowledge which imbues him and affects even the passing stranger with whom he comes into contact.

THE SYNAGOGUE AND ITS WORSHIP SERVICE

It is generally believed that the beginning of the synagogue occurred some time during the Babylonian exile (5th century B.C.). After the exile there seems to have been a broad development of the synagogue through Palestine and elsewhere where Jews settled in sufficient numbers. Though the synagogue seemed to originally have been a house of study, it became in time a house of prayer as well. Architecture of the synagogue varied throughout the centuries and no one style was necessarily preferred above the rest. In each century, that architectural mode was followed which generally prevailed at the time. Originally, it appears, women did not go in any numbers to synagogue services and so no special provisions were made for them in the ancient synagogues; that is, women were not permitted to worship in the same room with men. Eventually, it became customary to set aside an area for women. This space was separated from the main hall by a grating. This is still the custom in Orthodox synagogues today. In Reform synagogues, there is no separation between men and women. A strict interpretation of Exodus 20:4 rules out all carved images of living beings for use anywhere, but especially in places of worship. In antiquity, the only required equipment for a synagogue was a chest to contain the sacred scrolls (the Torah). In time it became a practice to cut out a niche for the Torah in the east wall. This receptacle is called the Holy Ark, an expression allusive of the Ark of the Covenant. At an early date, a platform was introduced for reading the Torah. A lamp called the Ner Tamid (eternal light) was hung before the Holy Ark and was kept burning constantly out of reverence for the Torah.

Worship in the synagogue, where Jews gathered to read the Law and to pray, was simply an extension of worship in the Temple. Anyone who went to the synagogue for the morning and evening services on the sabbath and feast days could legitimately think of himself as part of the assembly of the children of Israel at Jerusalem; he shared in their offerings, songs, and prayers.

The heart of the celebration in the synagogue was the reading of the Law, or Torah, that is, the Pentateuch. Jewish tradition chose to make Moses himself the origin of the service or readings. In thus putting the reading service under the patronage of the great law-giver, the intention was to bestow on it the dignity that stems from long duration. There were two forms of sequential reading of the Torah: the Palestinian cycle and the Babylonian cycle. The Palestinian cycle divided the reading of the Pentateuch to cover three years. The cycle in the Babylonian tradition, on the other hand, extended over only a single year. This tradition, probably of more recent origin than the Palestinian, supplanted the Palestinian in most Jewish communities.

When the people in the synagogue read the Torah, or five books of the Pentateuch, they were reading their own sacred history from its beginnings to the entry into the Promised Land. It is evident that a wide gulf separates our conception of history from that of Israel. We use ancient documents, the most objective we can find, to reconstruct the past. Israel does just the opposite. It starts with its own faith, and in the light of that it refashions and interprets the events of the past. The characteristic of Israel's contemplation of history is that it was a direct expression of her faith.

Because it was a direct expression of faith, it was transmitted from generation to generation like a family possession and retold from age to age.

> What we have heard and know, and what our fathers have declared to us, we will not hide from their sons; we will declare to the generations to come the glorious deeds of the Lord and his strength and the wonders that he wrought. He set it up as a decree in Jacob, and established it as a law in Israel, that what he commanded our fathers they should make known to their sons; so that the generation to come might know, their sons yet to be born, that they too may rise and declare to their sons that they should put their hope in God. (Psalm 78:3-6)

The reading of the Torah was not only a profession of faith but also an actualization of the ancient narratives for the benefit of the community. As it read its ancient history, Israel was fully involved; it was living its own history. This community was the people of whom the Torah was speaking. Together with the people of the Exodus, the Israel of a later day left Egypt, received the law at Mount Sinai, wandered across the desert, and entered the Promised Land. In every reading in the synagogue, the past lived in the present.

After the proclamation of the Law comes the Haftarah, or reading of the Prophets. From the ninth to the fourth century B.C. (the period of classical prophetism), the prophets shed their light upon the Law: commenting on it, reminding men of its requirements, making it relevant and topical for their brothers. The reasons why a reading from the Prophets was introduced into the synagogue service are not clear. It is assumed that this second reading was regarded as a commentary on or explanation of the Law, that showed its continuing relevance. It is highly unlikely that in the early days of the synagogue institution this second reading had any autonomous existence, it must have derived its value entirely from its relation to the Torah and provided the basis for the homily. Only much later did this reading itself take on the significance attached to the proclamation of God's word.

In order to assure that there would be a commentary on the Torah, the readings were chosen precisely for the light they could shed on the ancient texts. The reading of the Prophets did not have, in Jewish tradition, the same high place as the reading of the Law:

— The Law was read in its entirety and sequentially, in the form of passages chosen by tradition; the texts of the Prophets could be chosen freely by the reader.
— The reading of the Law was done by several readers; the reading of the Prophets, by one reader.
— The Law was translated verse by verse so that the community might hear the word of God in a strictly literal way; the prophets could be translated freely.
— The reading of the Law was obligatory at all services, even the weekday ones; the reading of the Prophets was not universally prescribed.

The homily in the synagogue service was inseparable from the reading of the Law and the Prophets. "Homily" here refers to the discourse explaining the word so as to make it more easily accessible to the community. This was a discourse with its own special characteristics; as such, it was to be found in no other religion or cultic service. For if Israel was a people brought into existence by the word, its celebrations could not but be essentially liturgies of the word, while the discourses pronounced in these celebrations inevitably concerned the veneration and explanation of the word. "This is what the Scripture says," or "This is what is written" — these were the usual formulas the speaker used in linking his explanation to the readings. They imposed on the speaker the obligation of constantly going back to the written text, drawing upon the word for what he had to say and making his human commentary a prolongation of the divine message. The usual form the homily took was a straightforward explanation of the word of God. The best example for the homily from this point of view is to be found in the assembly of Ezra: **"Ezra read plainly from the book of the law of God, interpreting it so that all could understand what was read"** (Nehemiah 8:8). Ezra read the Hebrew text and then translated it into Aramaic, the customary language of the time. The homily occurs after the reading of the Torah and the Prophets.

In present day worship services in Orhodox synagogues, also blessings and praise to Yahweh as well as the Psalms, form an integral part of the liturgy.

CIRCUMCISION

The rite of circumcision dates back to the time of Abraham. In a few terse sentences, Yahweh commanded Abraham to circumcise and called this rite the covenant between himself and his people (Genesis:17). The ceremony of circumcision is called Milah or sometimes Brit Milah, meaning "covenant of circumcision." The physical part of the ritual consists in cutting away the foreskin of the male child on the eighth day after birth. Circumcision is also called "the covenant of Abraham," to signify in this manner that Abraham showed his acceptance of God's covenant with him and his seed forever. Male converts to Judaism must also undergo circumcision. In biblical times and into the early Christian era, male slaves in Jewish families were circumcised. The Talmud forbids an uncircumcised person to participate in many Jewish rites such as eating the Paschal Lamb. In the history of Judaism, circumcision has always been a sign of fidelity to the religion of Abraham and Moses. It has also been the symbol to distinguish the Jew from the unbeliever. Part of the ceremony includes naming the Jewish boy, which follows right after the circumcision.

MOSES MAIMONIDES

Comparable to the Talmud in authority and in many respects more influential in shaping the mind of Judaism are the writings of the rabbinic sage Moses ben (son of) Maimon, known commonly as Moses Maimonides. Without exaggeration, Maimonides stands next to the prophet Moses, in the estimation of many Jews, as their greatest religious leader and the man whose wisdom produced the Judaism of modern times, even as Moses had shaped the religion of Israel centuries before Christ. "From Moses unto Moses," it was said, "there was none like Moses," meaning that in the twenty-five hundred intervening years (and since), from the prophet Moses, no one has more clearly assessed the genius of his people or more accurately expressed its spirit than Maimonides. He is the nearest to a prophet since the prophetic age of Israel. Born at Cordova, Spain, in 1135, Maimonides received a comprehensive education from his father, a learned Talmudist. During an anti- Jewish persecution by the Moslem Alhomades (1149), his family fled into exile and settled at Fez, the capital of Morocco.

In 1168 Maimonides finished his commentary on the Mishnah known as the Luminary. But a mind as original as his could not be satisfied with mere comment. He often boldly differed from the Talmud and especially rapped at errors and superstitions. His list of thirteen articles of faith is a synthesis of the Jewish religion and, to this day, a convenient standard of orthodoxy. Within a century of his death, this precis of belief was employed as a theme for synagogue poems in all countries of Jewish habitation.

In prose form Maimonides' articles are a condensation of the Talmud and of Judaic faith over ten centuries.

I believe with perfect faith that the Creator, praised be He, is the Creator and Guide of all creation, and that He alone has made, does make, and will make all things.

I believe with perfect faith that the Creator, praised be He, is a Unity, and that there is no unity like His in any manner, and that He alone is our God, who was, is and will be.

I believe with perfect faith that the Creator, praised be He, is not a body, and that He is free from all attributes of a body, and that He has no form whatsoever.

I believe with perfect faith that the Creator, praised be He, is the first and the last.

I believe with perfect faith that to the Creator, praised be He, and to Him alone is it proper to pray, and that it is not proper to pray to any besides Him.

I believe with perfect faith that all the words of the prophets are true.

I believe with perfect faith that the prophecy of Moses our great teacher, may he rest in peace, was true, and that he was the father of the prophets, both those who preceded and who followed him.

I believe with perfect faith that the entire Torah now in our possession is the same that was given to Moses our teacher, may he rest in peace.

I believe with perfect faith that this Torah will never be replaced, and that there will never be another Torah from the Creator, praised be He.

I believe with perfect faith that the Creator, praised be He, knows every deed of men and all their thoughts, as it is written, 'He fashions the hearts of them all and observes all their deeds.' (Psalm 33:15)

I believe with perfect faith that the Creator, praised be He, rewards those who keep His commandments and punishes those that transgress His commandments.

I believe with perfect faith in the coming of the Messiah, and though he tarry I will wait daily for him.

I believe with perfect faith that there will be a revival of the dead at a time when it shall please the Creator, praised be He, and exalted His fame for ever and ever.

According to Maimonides, only that person who recognizes the validity of these articles without analysis is a true Jew. Anyone who denies even one of them should have no part in the Jewish community.

ORIGIN OF MANKIND

Judaism has always believed that knowledge of the facts of creation comes exclusively from the Torah. Rabbinic theology holds that God created the world alone, with no one to help Him, out of nothing, and without effort or exertion. He created all things for His glory, and His cosmos, unlike that of creatures, does not undergo the ravages of time as may be seen from the enduring splendor of the heavens.

All living things in the original creation, according to the Talmud, came into being in their full maturity. Consistent with this position is the belief that Adam and Eve were created already in the full mental and physical perfection that others reach in adulthood.

Adam's original nature appeared extraordinary. He was gifted with a superb intelligence, capable of naming all the animals, of recognizing his own identity, and of addressing God as Lord. Before he offended his maker, Adam was so gifted he might have been mistaken for a god. He could listen to the voice of the Lord gladly and without fear, because he had not yet turned a deaf ear to Yahweh. God had personally urged him to be faithful, and promised him immortality. Had he remained faithful, he and Eve were destined to rule over the rest of creation. Sustained loyalty to God would have meant unspoiled happiness for him and all his descendants, with continued enjoyment of the delights of Eden. This theme pervades the Talmud, with the wistful reflection on a still innocent Adam and on the joys that might have been.

SIN

The Talmud uniformly teaches that sin began with the disobedience of Adam to the divine precept, and it has continued historically ever since. Equally uniform is the belief that the first transgression took the form of eating the fruit of some proscribed plant, though opinion varies on its precise nature. The general impression is that Adam's sin was extremely grave, that he was ungrateful to God, and brought death into the world where only life and happiness might have dwelled. What rabbinic theology does not say, and Judaism accordingly, is that because of Adam's sin all his posterity are sinners too. The sin of Adam was original, because it was the first. After him all other men have been sinners, but not because of any direct dependence on his transgression of the divine law.

Man's sinfulness, therefore, is seen rather as the result of his own personal deviation from the moral law, apart from any inherited sin as understood in traditional Christian thought. Yet the ancient rabbis also recognized that man had a strong proneness to evil. A popular theory, still in vogue among the Orthodox, is the idea that every person is born with an inclination to evil. Some say it enters man's nature as he leaves the womb; others claim it exists already in the womb. This evil is balanced, or at least coexistent, with a good impulse, but only after a child reaches adolescence, when he understands the responsibility of keeping the Torah.

SATAN

Satan, the fallen angel, existed before Adam. He used Eve to lead Adam into disobedience against God. The idea of a celestial fall of rebellious angels, before Adam, is certainly known in the Talmud. But it belongs exclusively to the apocalyptic Jewish tradition. The Talmud states that Satan, since the time of Adam, played the triple role of seducer, accuser, and destroyer of men. He seduces them into sin, then charges them before God, and finally, by divine permission, destroys them in punishment for their sins.

RECONCILIATION

Near the center of Jewish faith is the realization of God's sovereignty and man's need for reconciliation. For this reason Judaism's greatest holy day is not Passover but Yom Kippur, the Day of Atonement. Centuries before the Birth of Christ, Yom Kippur was already the holiest day of the year. Whether in Palestine or dispersed throughout the world, Jews fasted and prayed on that day as on no other day. On that one day each year all eyes turned to Jerusalem. Only on this day did the High Priest enter the Holy of Holies.

The High Priest normally performed the Temple rites. On Sabbath days and festivals, he showed himself to the people dressed in golden robes. But on Yom Kippur he became another man, a sinner like the rest of Israel. His prayers on that day were directed to the God of mercy, begging forgiveness for himself and the chosen race. For seven days before Yom Kippur, he left his home to live in the Temple. During that week he conducted the service alone, offered daily sacrifices, sprinkled the blood of the animals, burned the fragrant incense, and supervised the lighting of the Menorah. All of this was a prelude to the liturgy of the Great Day, to make sure that no mistake in word or gesture would be made in solemn acts of atonement to Yahweh. In the centuries since the destruction of the Second Temple, the Jews have not substantially changed the meaning of the Day of Atonement. With the Temple gone and bloody sacrifice no longer offered, there is no High Priest to preside and the Holy of Holies remains only a fond memory. But the spirit of the feast continues. Nowadays, the ritual of Atonement consists of three parts: spiritual confession of one's sins, physical offering of fowl (instead of a goat) or its equivalent in money, verbal affirmation of sorrow, and a plea for forgiveness. One of the most inspiring features of the Yom Kippur liturgy includes a long list of sins from which the Jew asks to be delivered. Fifty-three kinds of transgression are enumerated, each specific and each confessed in unison with other believers. Through the Yom Kippur liturgy runs a strong Messianic theme. Time and again, in prayer after prayer, the penitent looks forward to the hope of deliverance through the Anointed One.

Confession of sin to priests, and making satisfaction for them, is not of Christian origin. It is specifically commended in the Mosaic Law (Numbers 5:5-8). The Jewish priest could only make atonement for the guilty person and not forgive sin. Only God can forgive sins.

DIETARY LAWS

Hebrew dietary laws are meant to hallow a Jew's life. They recall that he lives under the discipline of the Law. Rabbinical tradition requires that animals be slaughtered by a Shohet, an expert slaughterer who must ensure the animal dies with the least possible pain and that blood is allowed to flow off freely. The cook, too, must observe certain regulations: the meat is cleansed and salted, so that every drop of blood will be drawn out. All vegetables are allowed to be eaten. Of the animal kingdom, only fish with scales and fins, certain kinds of fowl, and those quadrupeds that chew their food twice and have cloven hoofs are permitted. Meat and dairy product may not be eaten together; hence, two separate kinds of dishes are used, and a six hour interval must be observed between a meal with meat and one with milk or its derivatives. Reform Judaism has discarded the idea of kasrut (fitness), i.e., the laws regulating kosher food, although some of its adherents will, out of loyalty to parents or to the Jewish past, abstain from pork. While many observant Jews modify the strict requirements of the Law to suit demands of modern life, they expect their rabbis to observe, in their stead, the traditional rules uncompromisingly.

IMMORTALITY

Two main conceptions of human immortality trace their origin to Rabbinic Judaism: the essentially Hebrew idea of resurrection of the body, and the more Hellenistic notion of an immortal spirit.

Judaism acknowledges a belief in souls or spirits, as depicted in numerous passages of the Old Testament. Daniel, for example, teaches resurrection either to happiness or to punishment, according to one's conduct on earth. So too, portions of the Psalms, together with Job and Ecclesiastes, teach redemption of the soul from Sheol by the

Lord. Well before the Christian era, certainly Pharisaic Judaism recognized both aspects of immortality. If the Sadducees remained hostile to the idea of conscious survival after death, this lasted only as long as they had a temple and a voice in the religion of Israel. And all the while they were branded by their rivals as heretics.

In general, the Talmud offers little assurance of a blissful immortality to anyone but Jews. Israel is the heir of heaven or, at most, those who are Jewish proselytes. All Jews should have this hope as their birthright; yet they can exclude themselves for certain sins, including denial of the resurrection as taught in the Pentateuch. Individual Gentiles to whom salvation is conceded are usually described as having practiced extraordinary virtue or having been especially good to Jews or having abstained from forbidden food as prescribed in the Mosaic law.

In its understanding of immortality, Rabbinic Judaism defined afterlife practically, with a resurrected body rather than in terms of an immortal soul. Certainly rabbinic literature makes a distinction between body and soul. The soul of man first meant the breath which gives him life; it was the animating principle shared with lower organisms. Then soul came to mean the whole personality. Later Judaism differentiated between two aspects of personality: functions such as breathing, eating, and reproduction (in common with animals); and operations of a higher order like thought and affection by which one becomes aware of God and loves the Creator. This higher activity was attributed to the spirit. Some Talmudists spoke of the spirit as only the noblest part of the soul; others said it was separate. According to the first explanation, man's nature is a dichotomy of body and soul; on the second view, it shapes a trichotomy of body, soul, and spirit. The second view allowed for God's action on the soul beyond its native capacities.

While aware of all the subtleties of human nature, the Talmudists preferred to speak of immortal life apart from them, and simply talked about the resurrection of the body. They thereby left the impression that life after death would include the whole man, not just a part of him. Jews of the Orthodox persuasion still believe in a bodily resurrection from the dead.

FINAL JUDGEMENT

Only God can raise the dead. The Midrash explains this by referring to the opening of the graves (Ezekiel:37), adding that no one but He holds the key to human life. Following up on the suggestion of Hosea, the Midrash stated that resurrection will take place after three days. A Midrashic commentator says that this period is to be counted "from the beginning of the final judgement." Accordingly, death would mean lapsing into unconsciousness until being raised in final judgment. There is, however, another tradition which postulates immediate entrance at death into conscious immortal life, but this view is less common.

Punishment for the wicked in Ge-Hinnam (Greek: Gehenna) differs according to different writers in the Talmud. Some are annihilated. Others suffer with diminishing intensity for varying periods. Still others, very few, are consigned to eternal torments.

One of the clearest passages in the Talmud distinguishes three classes of persons at the final judgement: those entering Paradise immediately, those temporarily in hell (Purgatory), and those who suffer eternally.

Paradise, as the abode of the just after the resurrection, is an integral part of the Talmudic faith. It distinguishes clearly between the Messianic age and the world to come. In spite of occasional obscurity on the point, the Messianic age is simply a period of special worldly prosperity for Israel under a divinely chosen leader, whereas Paradise belongs to eschatology. It is the promise of unending joy after the sorrows and trials of this life.

Rabbinic Judaism describes two main views of heaven. The more spiritual explanation says that whatever people enjoy in the flesh in this life will have no place in the life to come. In that higher life there will be no eating, drinking, or procreation, and all the base emotions will be eliminated.

A more bodily theory teaches just the opposite. Paradise is one long celestial banquet, with food and drink, like people enjoy on earth — only greater abundance and producing greater satiety. A blissful privilege is the absence of any bad side effects, such as commonly associated with overindulgence.

The two attitudes are not uncommon in other religious traditions. What is perhaps unique is the close correlation between what a man did on earth and what he gets in the life to come. Merit and demerit, sometimes measured almost mathematically, are intrinsic to Talmudic eschatology.

INTERCESSION

"I believe," according to Maimonides, "that it is right to pray to the Creator and to Him alone, and it is not right to pray to any being besides Him." This injunction places man in immediate dependence on God alone and defines one of the most characteristic features of modern Judaism as distinct, say, from Christianity. No mediation is permissible or conceivable whether of a human being (like a priest) or of spiritual beings (like angels) or of a divinely authorized institution (like the Church). This a departure from pre-Christian Judaism which recognized the role of priests who offered sacrifice for the people as their intermediaries with God; who believed in the intercessory powers of angels, described in the rejected book of Tobias; and who accepted the mediatorial office of the great men of Israel to atone for the sins of their nation.

Maimonides' position is now practically uniform in the Jewish religion. No one less than God may be the object of prayer. No angel or priest, no saint or sacred institution should be considered as intermediaries between God and man, whereby mankind may approach closer to God. Only through the Deity Himself can our thoughts and emotions be sanctified.

MESSIANIC HOPE

Jews of every theological level look forward to a new era and expect a new age to dawn in which they will somehow be the divine instruments of redemption. Depending on how strong their biblical faith, this expectation is rooted in the predictions of a Messiah made by the ancient prophets.

Among Orthodox Jews, the Messianic hope is clear: God will one day send his Anointed One to earth. Indeed Judaism differs essentially from Christianity in this fact: that where the followers of Jesus of Nazareth believe He is the Messiah (Greek Christos), Jews are still waiting for the Mashijach (Hebrew for Anointed One) to come.

Opinions differ on the character of the Messiah. Several passages in the Talmud indicate that he is essentially the same as other men, though even then comparable to Abraham and Job. But a strong theme in rabbinic literature declares the Name of the Messiah existed before the world.

Maimonides cut through rabbinic speculation and gave the Jews a realistic picture of the Messianic age. The Messiah will certainly be a king of the house of David who will gather together the scattered people of Israel. But his coming will not radically change the course of human history.

King Messiah will arise and restore the kingdom of David to its former state and original sovereignty. He will rebuild the sanctuary and gather the dispersed of Israel. All the ancient laws will be reinstated in his days; sacrifices will again be offered; the Sabbatical and Jubilee years will again be observed in accordance with the commandments set forth in the Law. He who does not believe in the restoration or does not look forward to the coming of the Messiah denies not only teachings of the Prophets but also those of the Law of Moses, our teacher. (Minkin, World of Maimonides).

A careful distinction should be made, however, between the age of the Messiah and the final consummation of the world. The first will occur in this life, the second in the life to come.

All Israelites, their Prophets and Sages, longed for the advent of Messianic times, that they might have relief from the wicked tyranny that does not permit them properly to occupy themselves with the study of the Torah and the observance of the commandments; that they might have ease, devote themselves to getting wisdom, and thus attain to life in the World to Come. Because the King who will arise from the seed of David will possess more wisdom than Solomon and will be a great Prophet, approaching Moses, our teacher, he will teach the whole of the Jewish people and instruct them in the way of God; and all nations will come to hear him. The ultimate and perfect reward, the final bliss which will suffer neither interruption nor diminution is the life in the World to Come. The Messianic Era, on the other hand will be realized in this world; which will continue in its normal course except that independent sovereignty will be restored to Israel. The ancient Sages already said, 'The only difference between the present and the Messianic Era is that political oppression will then cease'. (Minkin, World of Maimonides).

There were prophecies predicting that the prophet Elijah would precede the Anointed One of the Lord. Maimonides warned, however, not to take these prophecies too literally.

The Anointed One to come will be recognized by his conduct. His lineage will be Davidic but only his virtue will give assurance that he is the one of whom David prophesied that of his loins would come the one to deliver Israel.

If there arise a king from the House of David who meditates on the Torah, occupies himself with the commandments, as did his ancestor David, observes the precepts prescribed in the Written and the Oral Law, prevails upon Israel to walk in the way of the Torah and to repair its breaches, and fights the battles of the Lord, it may be assumed that he is the Messiah. If he does things and succeeds, rebuilds the sanctuary on its site, and gathers the dispersed of Israel, he is beyond all doubt the Messiah. He will prepare the whole world to serve the Lord with one accord. (Minkin, World of Maimonides).

Challenged by Christianity, the Jews asked themselves what kind of person the Messiah was supposed to be, and whether he would perform such signs and wonders at least as great as the prophets of old. No, the One to come was not to be a miracle worker, nor should Israel anticipate such a deliverer. Obedience to the law, unchangeable, is the hallmark of Messiahship; peace and fidelity to Yahweh is the promise of the Messianic day.

Do not think that the Anointed King must give signs and miracles and create new things in this world, or bring the dead back to life, and the like. It will not be so. (Minkin, World of Maimonides).

But if there will be no physical portents announcing the Messianic age, there are promised changes in the moral order in the status of Israel with respect to Gentile nations. Said the Rabbis: "The sole difference between the present and the Messianic days is deliverance from servitude to foreign powers."

The sages and the prophets did not yearn for the days of the Anointed in order to seize upon the world, and not in order to rule over the heathen, or to be exalted by the peoples, or to eat and drink and rejoice, but to be free for the Torah and the wisdom within it, free from any goading and intrusion, so that they may be worthy of life in the coming world. When that time is here, none will go hungry, there will be no war, no jealousy and no conflict, for goodness will flow abundantly, and all delights will be plentiful as the numberless motes of dust, and the whole world will be solely intent on the knowledge of the Lord. Therefore those of Israel will be great sages, who know what is hidden, and they will attain what knowledge of their Creator it is in man's power to attain, as it is written, "For the earth shall be full of the knowledge of the Lord, as the waters cover the sea. [Isaiah 11:9] (Minkin, World of Maimonides).

Now that the nation of Israel is a reality, how do the Jews of strict observance look upon it, and how do their Messianic aspirations appear? The best index seems to be their current forms of liturgy, replete with invocations for the Messiah and, for the first time in two millennia, with prayers for the State of Israel.

It is impossible to read more than a dozen consecutive pages in the Hebrew Prayer Book for Sabbath and Festivals seeing an implicit reference to the Messiah and his kingdom. Certain features in these prayers predominate: the Messiah will be of the family of David, he will inaugurate a new era of peace for Israel, Jerusalem will be rebuilt, the ancient ritual will be reestablished, the expected deliverer will be the Anointed One, his character will be somehow transcendent, his advent must be prepared for by repentance and fervent petition and, in many prayers, the coming of the Messiah is connected (if not identified) with a mysterious coming of God himself.

SADDUCEEISM AND PHARISAISM

At the time of Jesus, two small but influential groups existed within Judaism, the Sadducees and the Pharisees.

The Sadducees did not believe in a future life, resurrection, or the immortality of the soul. They rejected the existence of angels and spirits as inconsistent with a thoroughgoing secularism. Yet they slavishly devoted themselves to the Written Law. The death penalty, they taught, should be inflicted for a host of "crimes," so that Sadducean morality became a byword for extreme severity.

Some historians dismiss the Sadducees as irrelevant to a proper understanding of Judaism today. It is said that their whole power and existence were bound up with the Temple worship. Upon the destruction of the Second Temple, they disappeared from Jewish life and history. A simplistic view of the Sadducees fails to take into account what Judaism has always been: a prophetic religion against which there have always been strong reactions among the Jews themselves. Sadducees typify the reaction of rationalism, which is uncomfortable with the concept of religion, notably as delineated in the Mosaic law. The inner tension in modern Judaism, especially in the United States, is unintelligible without taking this tendency into account. One cannot read a dozen pages by a Reform critic of Jewish Orthodoxy without sensing that the Sadducees have come back to life again.

Parallel with the Sadducees of ancient times dwelled the Pharisees, whose Hebrew name Perushim probably meant "set apart." A Pharisee avoided needless contact with others for reasons of ritual purity. Like the Sadducees their exact origin is unknown; also like them, they were a relatively narrow body closed to the masses. Though small in number they exercised great influence on the people whom they sought to inspire with their concept of holiness by propagating traditional religious teaching.

An impassable gulf separated the Pharisees from those ignorant of the Law or from those who did not observe the Law. The Pharisees would eat in groups among themselves, observing all the rules of purity that were binding on priests when they ate consecrated food in the Temple. They tried to extend their influence over the Temple at the expense of the Sadducees, whom they regarded as unbelievers. Not satisfied with the six hundred prescriptions of the Bible, they added numerous customs of their own, all to the dismay of the Sadducees. Between the two parties an antagonism grew that extended to every sphere of human conduct. As a rule, the Pharisees admitted the principle of evolution in their legal decisions, whereas the Sadducees seldom allowed the least adjustment to changing times.

In the popular mind, therefore, Pharisees were considered more lenient in their interpretation of the Law, while Sadducees were rigorists who clung to the exact wording of the written text. Moreover, the Pharisees placed the life of Israel within a framework of tradition (Oral Law) which they said was equally as vital as the Written Law (Bible). The Pharisaic doctrine of morality sought to embrace the whole life of the Jewish community, affecting the deepest question of human existence: the problem of good and evil, permanence of the human spirit, and the eschatology of man's destiny. What the Sadducees denied, the Pharisees affirmed: man did not die at death, his body would rise from the grave, the liberation of Israel would come under a personal Messiah, and the Day of Judgement would close this world of space and time only to begin the Kingdom of God that would never end.

The picture of Pharisaism as the ideal Jewish way of life sometimes differed from reality, since not all Pharisees lived up to these principles. The Talmud lists seven kinds of hypocrites, all Pharisees. If the vocabulary of Western culture still retains this image, picturing a deceitful man as a Pharisee, this should be put down to an accident of history. There were Pharisees who lived a double life. But Pharisaism itself was mainly responsible for strengthening the morality of post-Christian Judaism. It introduced a flexibility which allowed Jewish ethics to remain basically unchanged to this day. As such it is an integral part of historic Judaism.

CHAPTER 3
THE PATH TO JESUS CHRIST

By the time I met Irma in 1956 I had become lax in my religious practices. I stopped going regularly to the synagogue and following strict dietary laws as well as other required observances. Although I could not accept Reform Judaism, I had become a Reform Jew in practice. Yet, I still considered myself an Orthodox Jew because I believed in all the basic principles of that faith as described in chapter Z. During my years in high school and college my closest friends were Catholic. However, they had little influence on me before and during my conversion process. In fact, some of the Catholic beliefs, as expressed by them, turned me off. It was not until I studied Catholic teachings years later that I found out how many misconceptions they had about their faith and the Church's teachings.

In 1958, we bought our first house and moved together with our son Stephen to Wantagh, N.Y., on Long Island. I worked as an electronic engineer for a defense contractor. There I met Richard (Richy) Mercurio. Richy and his wife Frances became our closest friends. After I became a Catholic, I used to chide Richy for not being a better Catholic like Frances. Richy would say to me, "You know Charlie, I liked you better when you were a Jew."

My conversion process started in 1960 and increased in intensity during 1961. Looking back on those years, I see that conversion to Christ is not only a great gift from Him but also a mystery. In relating my conversion experience, I will tell how I came to know that Jesus was indeed the Messiah for whom I was waiting as a Jew. I will try to explain the logic and reasoning that led me to believe in Christ and eventually join the Catholic Church. What I find hard to explain is why what was to become so obvious to me is not obvious to others. I realize that many people are content to remain as they are and do not want, nor do they feel any need, to investigate or study other religions in the search for truth. Some who do search are held back because any change in their religion could have a devastating effect on their relationship with their family. I thank God all the time for allowing this Jew to come to know Him, and I pray to the Holy Spirit that my conversion story will be instrumental in helping others come to know Christ and His Church.

Early in 1960 Irma became pregnant. On November 21, 1960, she gave birth to our second child David via Caesarian section, the same as with our first child Stephen. David weighed almost 10 pounds. That afternoon at the hospital, the doctor confided the baby had a serious problem. When he tried to take him out of the incubator David would immediately get blue so he had to be put back. After I returned home the doctor called to tell me David had not improved. At 6 o'clock I went to the window, looked up to the sky now clear with bright shining stars, and prayed to God for my son. The following words came out of my mouth: "Jesus, if You are the Son of God, save my son." Why would a Jew who did not believe in Jesus, certainly not in His divinity, suddenly pray to Him for help? I could have asked Abraham or Moses for help. But I went to Jesus. Why? After my conversion I reflected on this scene, and came to realize it was not I who said that prayer, but God the Holy Spirit pleading to Jesus through me for my son. At 7 o'clock I went back to the hospital to see Irma and the baby. The doctor told me the baby had died an hour earlier, just about at the moment I had asked Jesus to save him. In the meantime Irma was unaware of what had happened. I was reluctant to tell her that evening the baby had died, because she had just undergone surgery in the morning. Although slightly sedated, she was happy and alert. I don't know how I kept the sad news from her. Yet I felt she detected something was wrong with the way I responded to her. What followed was the toughest night of my life. Mostly I prayed, shed tears, and felt very much alone. Stephen only three years old at the time, slept peacefully. The next morning I knew I had to tell a young mother that her child was dead. When I went into her room very early the next day and saw her, I broke down and cried as I told her the truth. It was a terrible day. Several days later Irma came home without her baby. The autopsy revealed David died because of a big hole in his heart. If the hole had been slightly smaller he could have lived and had surgery to correct the defect. I tried to ask God for answers. Neither Irma nor I blamed God. After his death, the baby was circumcised, given the name David, and buried in a Jewish cemetery.

In 1961, while visiting a library, something made me pick up a book on the life of Christ, take it home, and read it. This seemed strange because I was content with my Jewish beliefs and had thought about returning to the religious practices neglected for many years. This book showed me a side of Christ I never knew. He was loving and compassionate. Although He suffered greatly, He forgave those who were crucifying Him. Could this Man, Whom Christians believe is the Son of God, really be the Messiah of Israel prophesied in the Old Testament Scriptures? He certainly was a great man with great principles, Who claimed to be equal to God. But I read where a Catholic priest had said, "Jesus was either who He said He was, that is God, or the greatest liar that ever lived." For some unknown reason, I felt the need to look deeper into this mystery.

Also in 1961, I saw the movie "King of Kings," which depicts the life of Christ. I was unimpressed with the film. Although most Christians believe Jesus is God, this point failed to be conveyed to me in the movie. The movie offered little help to me. As I studied Christian beliefs, I reflected on the fact that it had been more than 2000 years since God sent a prophet to the Jews. In ancient times prophets like Jeremiah and Isaiah were sent to bring Jews who had strayed from the Law of Moses back to God. God was loving and merciful, always ready to forgive His chosen ones. Had the Jews become so holy and sinless that they needed no prophet until the Messiah comes? How can that be so, since most Jews today do not follow Mosaic Law, do not believe in the coming of the Messiah, nor in the resurrection of dead and the final judgement. Is it possible that there have been no more prophets because the Messiah (Jesus) had indeed come and Judaism failed to recognize Him?

As a Jew, I knew what Jews believed about the One God, the Messiah, the messianic age in this world, and life in the world to come after the Final Judgement. And I knew the Jewish arguments against the Trinity, and the Christian doctrines on the Messiah and eternity. But I wanted to learn from Christians the reasons for their beliefs. During this period of discovery in 1961 I relied on the Bible and sources which happened to be predominantly Catholic to find some answers. I had no problem with much of what Jesus taught or said because it was consistent with my Jewish beliefs. The complex process I undertook addressed the following three key issues:

1. That Jesus Who claimed to be the Messiah had to suffer and die.
2. Since as a Jew I believed in only one invisible God, how could the man Jesus claim equality with God? What about the reality of the concept of the Trinity?
3. The rise and growth of Christianity.

I can only attempt to briefly summarize how I came to the recognize that Jesus was indeed the Son of God and the Messiah of

Israel. During this period I did not speak to any Christian minister or priest about Christianity.

MESSIAH AS SUFFERING SERVANT

At the time of Jesus, Jews were awaiting a messiah that would restore Israel to its glory and deliver them from all their oppressors, especially the Romans. The prophet Isaiah in chapter 53 talks about an innocent man "who" was pierced through for our faults, crushed for our sins, and killed.

> Without beauty, without majesty (we saw him), no looks to at-tract our eyes; a thing despised and rejected by men, a man of sorrows and familiar with suffering, a man to make people screen their faces; he was despised and we took no account of him. And yet ours were the sufferings he bore, ours the sorrows he carried. But we thought of him as someone punished, struck by God, and brought low. Yet he was pierced through for our faults, crushed for our sins. On him lies a punishment that brings us peace, and through his wounds we are healed. We had all gone astray like sheep, each taking his own way, and Yahweh burdened him with the sins of all of us. Harshly dealt with, he bore it humbly, he never opened his mouth, like a lamb that is led to the slaughter-house, like a sheep that is dumb before its shearers never open-ing its mouth. By force and by law he was taken; would anyone plead his cause? Yes, he was torn away from the land of the liv-ing; for our faults struck down in death. They gave him a grave with the wicked, a tomb with the rich, though he had done no wrong and there had been no perjury in his mouth. Yahweh has been pleased to crush him with suffering. If he offers his life in atonement, he shall see his heirs, he shall have a long life and through him what Yahweh wishes will be done. His soul's an-guish over he shall see the light and be content. By his sufferings shall my servant justify many, taking their faults on himsel Hence I will grant whole hordes for his tribute, he shall divide the spoil with the mighty, for surrendering himself to death and letting himself be taken for a sinner, while he was bearing the faults of many and praying all the time for sinners. (Isaiah 53:2-12)

The life of Christ, especially His passion, appears to match that of the suffering servant in Isaiah. The Gospels also identify the suf-fering servant as Christ. Since there was no notion in Judaism that the Messiah had to suffer and die, how does it address that servant in Isaiah 53? Hebrew scholars say Isaiah was referring to the nation

Israel. After reflecting and praying on this, the Jewish notion of nation made no sense. I came to see, as pointed out by Christian biblical scholarship, that Isaiah was speaking of a man. And that Man was Christ.

TRINITY

In chapter 2 I pointed out that Judaism rejected the concept of trinity because to Jews it represented belief in three gods and denied the belief in one God. But christians point out they also believe only in one God, One Who is three persons and not three gods. It is a great mystery. In the Gospel of John, Jesus claims He and the Father are one. Jesus promises to send His Spirit to the Church. He also commissions the Apostles to baptise in the Name of the Father, Son, and Holy Spirit. Is it possible that the concept of three persons in one God is implicit in the Old Testament Scriptures?

In Old Testament Scriptures a developing theme recurs on the Word and Wisdom of God. God creates by His Word and Creation manifests His Wisdom. The Word of God is both power and revelation. Word is power because it effects what it says and is revelation because it reveals God. The Old Testament Scriptures show a great development of the literary personification of the Word and Wisdom of God. In Psalm 33:6 the reader cannot distinguish Word from God. Metaphors such as the breath of God (i.e., it breathes His power) are used.

> **By the word of Yahweh the heavens were made, their whole array by the breath of His mouth.** (Isaiah 33:6)

In Psalm 107:20 word becomes distinct from God (strictly literary personification).

> **Then they called to Yahweh in their troubles and He rescued them from their sufferings, sending His word and curing them, He snatched them from the pit.** (Psalm 107:20).

In Isaiah 55:10-11 the Word goes forth, brings power, and effects the will of God.

> **...so the word that goes from My mouth does not return to me empty, without carrying out my will and succeeding in what it was sent to do.** (Isaiah 55:11)

The Old Testament books of Proverbs, Wisdom, and Sirach (Ecclesiasticus) show more interest in literary personification of the Wisdom of God. As mentioned in chapter 2, the books of Wisdom and Sirach, which are part of the Septuagint, are not part of the Jewish or Protestant Canon of the Old Testament. (See heading Bible, chapter 2.)

In chapter 8 of the book of Proverbs, Wisdom speaks of being the architect of Creation Who worked at God's side.

Yahweh created me when his purpose first unfolded, before the oldest of his works. From everlasting I was firmly set, from the beginning, before earth came into being. The deep was not, when I was born, there were no springs to gush with water. Before the mountains were settled, before the hills, I came to birth; before he made the earth, the countryside, or the first grains of the world's dust. When he fixed the heavens firm, I was there, when he drew a ring on the surface of the deep, when he thickened the clouds above, when he fixed fast the springs of the deep, when he assigned the sea its boundaries — and the waters will not invade the shore — when he laid down the foundations of the earth, I was by his side, a master craftsman, delighting him day after day, ever at play in his presence, at play everywhere in his world, delighting to be with the sons of men. (Proverbs 8:22-31)

In the book of Ecclesiasticus (Sirach), Chapter 24:1-14, we read the following autobiographical discourse of Wisdom:

Wisdom speaks her own praises, in the midst of her people she glories in herself She opens her mouth in the assembly of the Most High, she glories in herself in the presence of the Mighty One; I came forth from the mouth of the Most High, and I covered the earth like mist. I had my tent in the heights, and my throne in a pillar of cloud. Alone I encircled the vault of the sky and I walked on the bottom of the deeps. Over the waves of the sea and over the whole earth, and over every people and nation I have held sway. Among all these I searched for rest, and looked to see in whose territory I might pitch camp. Then the creator of all things instructed me, and he who created me fixed a place for my tent. He said, 'Pitch your tent in Jacob, make Israel your inheritance'. From eternity, in the beginning, he created me, and for eternity I shall remain. (Ecclesiasticus 24:1-14)

In the book of Wisdom, chapter 10:15 depicts Wisdom delivering Israel from Egypt.

A holy people and a blameless race, this she delivered from a nation of oppressors. (Wisdom 10:15)

Chapter 18:14-17 explains that the Word delivers Israel from Egypt.

When peaceful silence lay over all, and night had run the half of her swift course, down from the heavens, from the royal throne, leapt your all-powerful Word; into the heart of a doomed land the stern warrior leapt. Carrying your unambiguous command like a sharp sword, he stood, and filled the universe with death; he touched the sky, yet trod the earth. Immediately, dreams and gruesome visions overwhelmed them with terror, unexpected fears assailed them. (Wisdom 18:14-17)

Therefore, it can be deduced Wisdom and Word are one and the same.

In Proverbs 8:32-36 we read of Wisdom's great invitation:

And now, my sons, listen to me; listen to instruction and learn to be wise, do not ignore it. Happy those who keep my ways! Happy the man who listens to me, who day after day watches at my gates to guard the portals. For the man who finds me finds life, he will win favor from Yahweh; but he who does injury to me does hurt to his own soul, all who hate me are in love with death. (Proverbs 8:32-36)

Jews imply that this personification of Word and Wisdom means the Torah. (See Torah chapter 2.) In fact the rabbis state:

1. Torah existed before the creation and lay in the bosom of God.
2. World was created by the Torah.
3. World was created for the sake of the Torah.
4. Study of Torah is the way to life.

St. John, an Apostle of Christ and a Jew, transfers what is attributed to the Torah by the rabbis to Christ in the Prologue of his Gospel:

In the beginning was the Word: the Word was with God and the Word was God. He was with God in the beginning. Through him all things came to be, not one thing had its being but through him. All that came to be had life in him and that life was the light

of men, a light that shines in the dark, a light that darkness could not overpower. (John 1:1-5)

The Word was made flesh, he lived among us, and we saw his glory, the glory that is his as the only Son of the Father, full of grace and truth. (John 1:14)

Then I saw the real meaning of Proverbs 8:32-36 (see above) in John 14:6, where St. John records Jesus saying:

I am the Way, the Truth, and the Life. (John 14:6)

In John's Gospel the "Word" is used only in the Prologue. In the remainder of the Gospel, Jesus is the revelation of God and John uses Wisdom literature from the Old Testament. The Gospel of John contains all the elements of the Trinity doctrine. From then on, I was unable to accept the rabbis' notion of the Torah as stated above.

The Old Testament relates the many times Israelites turned away from God and His Law. Yet the God of love and mercy would always reach down to His sinful people by sending His prophets to pull them back to Him. Were it not possible that finally, because of His infinite love and mercy, God sends Jesus His only begotten Son to redeem His people? The struggle within me regarding the nature of God was intense, but the Christian understanding of the nature of God began to make sense to me.

The teachings of Jesus the Messiah are an acknowledgment and not a denial of God's oneness as stressed in Judaism's expression of faith proclaimed in the Shema:

Hear, O Israel, the Lord Our God, the Lord is One.
(Deuteronomy 6:4)

The eternal Law in the Shema is more fully expressed in the Trinity, for it tells us that the One God manifests as the Creator, the Redeemer, and the Sanctifier without impairing His oneness. As a Jew I did not properly realize that Christians are monotheists, not polytheists; that Christians believe in the one true God, and only one; that He is the God of Abraham, Isaac, and Jacob; that He functions as three distinct persons - Father, Son, and Holy Spirit. Unity and plurality of the existence of the One True God are inferred in the first chapter of the Bible. Therein we learn that when God made man, He referred to Himself twice, in the plural:

Let us make man in our own image, in the likeness of ourselves...
(Genesis 1:26)

Three distinct persons are named in the Godhead by Isaiah: "God the eternal," "God the Spirit," and "Lord the Redeemer". To quote the Old Testament:

...and all the time these things have been happening, I have been present. - And now the Lord Yahweh, with his spirit, sends me. Thus **says Yahweh, your redeemer, the Holy One of Israel...** (Isaiah 48:16-17)

Underlying these passages is the realization on the part of many Jews that accepting belief in the Trinity carries with it belief in Jesus as the Messiah, the Second Person of the Triune God. Those Jews who have been blest with the grace of seeing and believing in God in His Tri-unity have been elevated from the severity of the Jewish concept of Him as a Ruler to the love of God as a Father, Sacrificing Son, and a Sanctifying Spirit.

THE RISE OF CHRISTIANITY

More than one billion Christians inhabited the world in 1961. A Jew named Jesus and His twelve Jewish followers started Christianity. Jesus claimed to be the long awaited Jewish Messiah. But Jews, including His apostles, never conceived that the Messiah would be God and would suffer and die. After Jesus' death, His disciples claimed that He rose from the dead and then after 40 days ascended to Heaven to sit at God's right hand (in rabbinical language this meant equality with God). On the Jewish feast of Pentecost they claimed God's Holy Spirit came upon them and they went out to preach about Jesus. Now the apostles were not from the Jewish elite. They were ordinary men not especially skillful or gifted. Yet they converted many Jews to Christ. The first Christian community, made up of all Jews, lived together lovingly, as described in the Acts of the Apostles:

These remained faithful to the teachings of the apostles, to the brotherhood, to the breaking of the bread and to the prayers. The many miracles and signs worked through the apostles made a deep impression on everyone. The faithful all lived together and owned everything in common; they sold their goods and possessions and shared out the proceeds among themselves according to what each one needed. They went as a body to the Temple

> every day but met in their houses for the breaking of bread; they shared their food gladly and generously; they praised God and were looked up to by everyone. Day by day the Lord added to their community those destined to be saved. (Acts 2:42-47)

That Jews, or anyone for that matter, could form this kind of community amazed me. Then, along comes Paul, a fanatical and learned Pharisee, sees Christ in an apparition, and starts converting pagans. At this time in history there were no rapid transit systems, radios, televisions, telephones, and newspapers. Yet within 30 years after the death of Jesus, thousands of Christians suffered persecution and death for their belief. This sect continued to grow over the next several hundred years in spite of brutal persecution. What logical explanation could there be for this growth? Why didn't this movement die in its infancy? If Jesus was an impostor and did not have God on His side, how could His followers have been so effective? And how could God allow His people to be so misled, not to mention millions of others over the centuries?

In the previous chapter on Jewish Belief I discussed what Jews believed would happen when the Messiah comes. They believe the coming of the messianic age (i.e., restoration of temple worship, peace, no suffering) would come about without miraculous intervention. Anybody living in this century who believes that an age of peace and tolerance and an end to suffering, could happen without some great miraculous intervention by God should seek psychiatric counsel. By Christmas of 1961 I reached the conclusion that God indeed had been behind the growth of Christianity because it presented the Truth. I may have reached that conclusion a few months earlier if I had read in the book of Acts, chapter 5:27-39:

> When they had brought them in to face the Sanhedrin, the high priest demanded an explanation. 'We gave you a formal warning,' he said, 'not to preach in this name, and what have you done? You have filled Jerusalem with your teaching, and seem determined to fix the guilt of this man's death on us.' In reply Peter and the apostles said, 'Obedience to God comes before obedience to men; it was the God of our ancestors who raised up Jesus, but it was you who had him executed by hanging on a tree. By his own right hand God has now raised him up to be leader and savior, to give repentance and forgiveness of sins through him to Israel. We are witnesses to all this, we and the Holy Spirit whom God has given to those who obey him. This so infuriated them that they wanted to put them to death. One member of the

Sanhedrin, however, a Pharisee called Gamaliel, who was a doctor of the Law and respected by the whole people, stood up and asked to have the men taken outside for a time. Then he addressed the Sanhedrin, 'Men of Israel, be careful how you deal with these people. There was Theudas who became notorious not so long ago. He claimed to be someone important, and he even collected about four hundred followers; but when he was killed, all his followers scattered and that was the end of them. And then there was Judas the Galilean, at the time of the census, who attracted crowds of supporters; but he got killed too, and all his followers dispersed. What I suggest, therefore, is that you leave these men alone and let them go. If this enterprise, this movement of theirs, is of human origin it will break up of its own accord; but if it does in fact come from God you will not only be unable to destroy them, but you might find yourselves fighting against God. (Acts 5:27-39)

In 1961 Irma and I sold our house and bought a new one in Commack, NY. While our new home was being completed, we moved in temporarily with Irma's parents in Brooklyn, NY. On Christmas Eve 1961 I decided to watch midnight Mass on television broadcast from St. Patrick's Cathedral in New York City. During the consecration, as the Bishop elevated the Consecrated Host, I looked at It and said, "My Lord and my God." Instantly all the tensions within me disappeared and I felt at peace. Everything I had read and studied about Jesus became crystal clear. No doubting or wandering anymore! Jesus was my Savior and my God. St. Paul experienced an instant conversion when He saw Jesus in person on his way to Damascus. I also became a convert to Christ when I saw Him in the Eucharist. It was the same Christ Paul had seen. From that moment I knew that Jesus was God and the Messiah I had been anticipating, and that He was and is present in the Eucharist.

I didn't wait for the Mass to end to tell Irma of my experience. She didn't reply because I think she was in shock. Although Irma knew of the many months I had spent reading and studying about Christianity, she believed it was only a passing fad. A few days later when I called her from work and told her I contemplated being baptised, she broke down and cried. She feared for our relationship and what the family would say and do. Because she was troubled I assured her I would do nothing, but I couldn't change the belief in my heart. I rapidly descended from the heights I attained just a few nights earlier. Early in 1962 I moved my family to Commack, NY. In February 1962 Irma and I went to her cousin's house for dinner. I told her relatives about my spiritual experience of the previous year and how I came to believe in Christ. Although Jews they knew very little about Judaism and did not practice it. Still they tore me apart for believing in Christ. As we drove home Irma told me she was furious with her family because of the way they treated me and said it would be okay with her if I were baptized and joined a church.

CHAPTER 4
THE ROAD TO THE CATHOLIC CHURCH

After accepting Jesus as my Lord and God, I faced the important decision of choosing a church. The existence of so many Christian churches, each with its own structure and understanding of the Gospel, overwhelmed me. As a Jew I found it difficult to believe that God would send His Son to create many different Christian Churches.

Jesus intended only one Church founded on the "Rock," Peter. At the Last Supper Jesus prayed to the Father:

> **May they all be one Father; may they be one in Us as You are in Me and I am in You, so that the world may believe it was You Who sent Me.** (John 17:21)

Men, not God, created the divisions. Divisions within Christianity, which many times include brutal hostility among the Churches, is a scandal and an obstacle to belief in Jesus Christ. By October 1962 I had completed my study and believed that the Catholic Church was indeed the one true Church founded by Christ.

If the Catholic Church is truly the fulfillment of ancient Judaism, then it should possess characteristics similar to those of the ancient faith. What then was ancient Judaism? Judaism was a revealed religion with God-ordained faith, worship, and way of life. As an organic religion, Judaism dated from Moses, the law-giver, through whom God instituted the religious and civil requirements of the Israelites. The Torah and the other inspired, prophetical writings in the Old Testament set forth Judaism, pure and unadulterated. Based also upon the Oral Law, God is said to have communicated to Moses with the Commandments, but which Jews did not reduce to writing during the priest-functioning ages of Israel. Hence Orthodox Judaism today, like Catholicism, holds that the source of revelation is both the written and the unwritten word of God, contained in both Scripture and Tradition. Judaism's first principle professed belief in a transcendent, eternal God, Whose oneness is stressed in its universal expression of faith. Ancient Judaism was also a priestly religion. Our Lord said to the Jews,

> Do not imagine that I have come to abolish the Law or the Prophets. I have come not to abolish but to complete them. I tell you solemnly, till heaven and earth disappear, not one dot, not one little stroke, shall disappear from the Law until its purpose is achieved. Therefore, the man who infringes even one of the least of these commandments and teaches others to do the same will be considered the least in the kingdom of heaven; but the man who keeps them and teaches them will be considered great in the kingdom of heaven. (Matthew 5:17-19)

The remaining sections of this chapter summarize the spiritual basis that led me to the Catholic Church.

THE POPE AND INFALLIBILITY

After destruction of the Temple and disappearance of the Jewish priesthood, Jews accepted the authority of the Talmud as their guide until the messiah comes. A Jew can not decide on his own authority or that of some rabbi, what he should or should not believe and how to live his faith.

When Simon Peter professed the Divinity of Christ, Jesus promised him Supreme Leadership of the Kingdom of Heaven on Earth.

> When Jesus came to the region of Caesarea Philippi he put this question to his disciples, 'Who do people say the Son of Man is? And they said, 'Some say he is John the Baptist, some Elijah, and others Jeremiah or one of the prophets.' 'But you' he said 'who do you say I am?' The Simon Peter spoke up, 'You are the Christ, the Son of the living God.' Jesus replied, 'Simon, son of Jonah, you are a happy man! Because it was not flesh and blood that revealed this to you but my Father in heaven. So now I say to you: You are Peter and on this rock I will build my Church. And the gates of the underworld can never hold out against it. I will give you the keys of the kingdom of heaven: whatever you bind on earth shall be considered bound in heaven; whatever you loose on earth shall be considered loosed in heaven.' Then he gave the disciples strict orders not to tell anyone that he was the Christ. (Matthew 16:13-20)

Based on this Scripture passage the Catholic Church holds that Christ, Who is the Eternal Rock, the inward and invisible foundation of His Church, selected Peter as the secondary rock upon which

He would build His visible Church. Christ is the Good Shepherd, yet He selected Peter to be the shepherd of His flock:

"Feed My lambs,"...."look after My sheep" (John 21:16-17)

That Simon was selected by Jesus to be the rock foundation of His Church, is enforced by the unquestioned fact that the "keys of the kingdom" were promised to him on the occasion when his name was changed from Simon to Peter. The keys signify power, authority, jurisdiction, such as exercised by every Bishop of Rome from Peter to the present. Jesus gave strict orders to His disciples not to tell anyone He was the Christ, because it would take the Holy Spirit coming on Pentecost to enlighten the Apostles and disciples as to Who Jesus really was and provide meaning to what He had said. At the Last Supper Jesus told the Apostles,

But the Advocate, the Holy Spirit, whom the Father will send in My name will teach you everything and remind you of all I have said to you. (John 14:26)

Christ's Church, which is His Mystical Body, may be likened to a corporation, differing from a legal corporation in its indestructibility, Divinely established to exist during all time, and therefore not capable of being dissolved. A corporation is a society made up of individuals who act as a single legal person. Once established, it is self-perpetuating. Vacancies caused by death or other circumstances, are filled, and its numbers increased, without injury to its corporate existence. A legal corporation abides by the laws of the state and is therefore a creature of the state; the Divine Corporation is the creature of the Son of God. Christ called this Divine Corporation His household (Matthew 10:25), His flock (Matthew 26:31), His Church (Matthew 16:18); it is referred to thirty-six times in Matthew's Gospel as the "kingdom." Such a household, flock, kingdom, or Church must have someone who ranks first in authority, who has primacy — the first rank. That person is Peter, Whom Christ Himself appointed. The continuance of that Corporation until the "consummation of the world" necessitated successors, who would continue to exercise that primary function. The Catholic Church designated these heads as popes.

The belief that the Church cannot be led astray from the truth when it believes and defines a doctrine under the guidance of the Holy Spirit is called infallibility. By promising He would be with the Church until the end of time He ensured its structure would be infallible until His return.

> **And know that I am with you always; yes, to the end of time.** (Matthew 28:20)

The Catholic Church teaches infallibility may be expressed in three ways:

1. The Pope alone, in specific circumstances, can speak with the gift of infallibility. The first Vatican Council in 1870 defined when and how the Pope spoke infallibly. The Second Vatican Council (1962-1965) substantially repeated this doctrine in the Dogmatic Constitution on the Church:

> **This is the infallibility which the Roman Pontiff (the Pope), the head of the college of bishops, enjoys in virtue of his office, when, as supreme shepherd and teacher of all the faithful, who confirms his brethren in their faith (cf. Luke 22:32), he proclaims by a definitive act some doctrine of faith or morals. Therefore his definitions, of themselves, and not from the consent of the church, are justly styled irreformable, for they are pronounced with the assistance of the Holy Spirit, an assistance promised to him in blessed Peter... For then the Roman Pontiff is not pronouncing judgement as a private person. Rather, as the supreme teacher of the universal Church, as one in whom the charism of the infallibility of the church herself is individually present, he is expounding or defending a doctrine of Catholic faith. (no. 25)**

The definition makes it clear the Pope speaks infallibly only when he proclaims by a definitive act some doctrine concerning faith or morals. This quotation clarifies that the Pope is not speaking infallibly on every occasion.

2. Christian truth can be stated infallibly by the Bishops of the Church, in union with the Pope.

> **The infallibility promised to the Church resides also in the body of bishops when that body exercises supreme teaching authority with the successor of Peter. To the resultant definitions the assent of the Church can never be wanting, on account of the activity of that same Holy Spirit, whereby the whole flock of Christ is preserved and progresses in unity of faith. (no. 25)**

3. The church as a whole is infallible when it recognizes and agrees upon a truth in the sphere of faith and morals. As the Dogmatic Constitution on the Church of Vatican II pronounced:

> **The body of the faithful as a whole, anointed as they are by the Holy One** (cf. I John 2:20,2 7), **cannot err in matters of belief Thanks to a supernatural sense of the faith ("sensus fidei") which characterizes the people as a whole, it manifests this unerring quality when 'from the bishops down to the last member of the laity,' it shows universal agreement in matters of faith and morals.** (no. 12)

Of course, to determine what all the faithful in the world believe remains a difficult problem.

It needs to be noted that although the Pope and the Bishops in union with him, have the gift of infallibility, it does not guarantee these men are also holy. History records that Popes and Bishops have at times been brutal and have not reflected Christian virtues in their behavior. They do not automatically attain eternal life. They are sinners like all people, in need of God's mercy and forgiveness.

Christ bestowed special dignities upon Peter before and after he denied Christ. Does the denial of Peter militate against the fact that Christ made Simon, in name and office, the rock upon which He built His Church?; that to him He delegated His authority, symbolised by the "keys"?; that Christ the Good Shepherd, selected Peter to shepherd His lambs and sheep? In the Old Testament we see Aaron selected by God as the first high priest, the Peter of the Old Law, despite Aaron's violation of His law, by setting up a golden calf. This apparent idolatry caused Moses, with warranted anger, to break the Tables of the Law, and to destroy the golden idol (Exodus 32). Aaron repented for his sin, and Moses gained forgiveness for him from Almighty God. Peter repented, and Christ, the God-man, looked at Peter, and forgave him. We must never forget that God is merciful, and therefore forgives repentant sinners. Recall to mind King David, the adulterer and murderer, who repented and became God's beloved, and from whose family came the Christ.

REVELATION

Most Protestant Christians hold firmly that Scripture is the sole source and rule of Christian belief. They do not accept any teaching or doctrine not in the Bible. At the time of Jesus there existed in Israel both the Written Law (the Scriptures) and the Oral Law (Tradition). Jewish beliefs, such as the coming of the Messiah and the resurrection of the dead, come from Tradition and not from explicit passages in the Scriptures. Jesus used both the Scriptures and Tradition to prove He was the promised Messiah. While Jesus lived, He never told anyone to record what He said or did. Jesus did not leave a book for Christians that provided all His commandments, teachings, and guidance as to how we should live and worship God. He called us to be the people of God (community) filled with the Holy Spirit. The Holy Spirit would transmit His revelation and its implications to us in the same way as in Old Testament days, through the Scriptures and Tradition. The list of authenticated writings along with the Old Testament is called the Canon of Scripture, and that collection of writings is called the Bible.

The formation of the New Testament Canon, like that of the Old, developed gradually; it was not produced all at one time as a completed whole. The first writings of the New Testament included separate, independent writings, called into being at different times, in different circumstances, to meet various needs. There was no intention on the part of the Apostles and their disciples of collaborating in the production of a common work to be left as a legacy. Our Lord and His Apostles were teachers rather than writers; they taught and preached the Word of God, as in St. Paul's words, **"Faith comes by hearing"** (Romans 10:17).

The written word conveyed an additional means of spreading the Gospel. In the first two centuries of the Church many Christian communities were already in existence and yet did not possess all the writings in circulation at the time. The Canon of the Old Testament was firm by the fifth century despite some questioning by scholars. All the New Testament books too were generally known. Religious authorities acknowledged most of them as inspired by the end of the second century. Prior to the end of the fourth century, a controversy loomed over the inspired character of several New Testament works. Controversy ended during the fourth century and all books in the Old Testament and New Testament were enumerated in the Canon stated by the Councils of Hippo (393 A.D.) and Carthage (397 A.D.), and affirmed by Pope Innocent I in 405 A.D. The Council of Trent solemnly defined the Canon of the Bible in 1546.

As a Jew, I was taught God's word comes to us through Scripture and Tradition. The same is true in the Catholic Church. I find it odd for people to believe that only Scripture is the Word of God, because nowhere in the Bible does it state that these specific books (and only these books) are the inspired Word of God. Then, on whose authority is the Bible truly God's word? It does not take much "brain power" for us to realize that without a living, Divinely instituted authority there is no way of knowing, with certitude, whether the writings in the Bible were inspired by God, or what those writings really mean. Therefore, the most manifest sign of true wisdom for Catholics, in matters religious and moral, is listening to the Voice of Christ expressed through the Divinely guaranteed "brains" of the Church of Christ. For Catholics the "brains" include the Bishops, who are successors of the Apostles; in union with the Pope, the successor of Peter.

WORSHIPAND PRIESTHOOD

Ancient Judaic worship centered on public sacrifice, homage paid to God, through priests, covered sin, guilt, peace, thanks, and other offerings. Before God gave the Law through Moses to Israel, Adam and his sons, Abraham and his posterity, and Melchizedek each offered sacrifices because all were priests and ministers of their own sacrifices. But with Moses came the delegation of that function and power, by Divine command, to Aaron and his family descendants, the Aaronic priesthood. Aaron was the elder brother of Moses and his spokesman, for Moses was slow of speech and lacked eloquence. Aaron the Supreme Pontiff of the Jews, and Peter, the same for Christians, were both Divinely selected. God selected Aaron, who belonged to the tribe of Levi, in a miraculous way, to offer the Sacrifice of the Altar and act as mediator between Jews and God. Chapter 17, Book of Numbers tells the story of Aaron's selection as the first High Priest of the Jews. Aaron and his sons formed that Divine priesthood of the Old Law (Exodus 28). With the consecration of Aaron (by Moses) the tribe of Levi, to which Aaron belonged, was separated into two divisions; Kohanim (priests), who functioned at the Altar, and Levites (servitors), who assisted in the service of the tabernacle and Temple. One of the high priest's functions was to enter the Holy of Holies, once a year (Yom Kippur Day), and sprinkle the blood of the sin-offering on the mercy seat while incense burned within the Veil (Exodus 16). The high priest also presided over the Court of Judgement, and consulted the Divine oracle.

The Aaronic priesthood, the Mosaic sacrifices, and the Temple of Jerusalem exist no more. They came to an end during the first century A.D. Judaism without a priesthood is no longer the religion it was, of God, than the Catholic religion would be today without its priesthood. Mosaic Judaism ended over nineteen centuries ago, with the fulfillment of its prophecies in the birth, life, works, death, and resurrection of the promised Messiah. Christianity became the reality, completion, and fulfillment that Judaism foreshadowed.

Malachi, the last of Israel's prophets, in the fifth century before Christ, told of the end of Jewish sacrifices; that the name of God honored among the Jews would be "great among the Gentiles," that the sacrifice offered in but one place would be offered all over the world and that it would be a "clean oblation," as in the Mass (Malachi 1:11).

> **But from farthest east to farthest west my name is honored among the nations and everywhere a sacrifice of incense is offered to my name, and a pure offering too, since my name is honored among the nations, says Yahweh Sabaoth.** (Malachi 1:11)

The priests of Israel offered sacrifices at but one altar, in the Temple of Jerusalem. These sacrifices comprised bloody offerings (Leviticus Chapters 1-7). The Mass is called a sacrifice as declared by the Council of Trent

> **The same Christ (offered on Calvary) is present (mystically) and immolated in an unbloody manner Who once for all offered Himself in a bloody manner on the altar of the cross.**

The Mass depicts the Passion of our Lord, unfolding, from the agony in the Garden of Gethsemane to the offering of Christ Himself upon the Cross for redemption of mankind. The central act in the Mass is enacted when the priest, as the representative of Christ, takes up the unleavened bread and the wine, and says the words which Christ commanded to be said **"in remembrance"** of Him: **"This is My Body — This is My Blood."** Then the bread and wine become in substance the Body and Blood of Christ. Christ Himself is present under the appearance or species of bread and wine. This Eucharistic Sacrifice is offered by Catholic and Orthodox priests on altars throughout the world.

Catholics believe God created only two priesthoods. One, which began with Aaron, exists no more; the other, which began with Jesus Christ, displaced the Aaronic priesthood. Hence, only one priesthood of God exists. It is a continuation of Christ in His Catholic Church. St. Paul tells us in his letter to the Hebrews of a new priesthood superior to the Levitical priesthood, not based on physical descent.

Table I summarizes some of the roles of the priests of Israel and of Catholic priests.

Table I — Similarities Between Israel and Catholic Priests	
Priests of Israel	**Catholic Priests**
Hereditary. Aaron and his male descendants.	Men who meet the moral, physical, and intellectual requirements of the Church without regard to their genealogical connection.
High Priest selected on the principles of primogeniture. High priest is supreme in authority.	One High priest only, Jesus Christ, the Son of God. Priest who is Bishop of Rome supreme authority.
High Priest is president of the Sanhedrin, the supreme council of the Jewish people.	Pope (Bishop of Rome) is head of all Ecumenical (world) councils.
High priest offered principal sacrifices, being only person permitted to enter the Holy of Holies.	All priests offer Sacrifice.
Principal sacrifices were bloody offerings.	An unbloody offering a "clean oblation."
Sacrifices offered at but one altar, in the Temple of Jerusalem.	Sacrifice offered on altars in all nations.
Teach and interpret the Law.	Teach and interpret the Law that is still binding and the Gospels.
Teach the Children of Israel the Mosaic ordinances.	Teach what Jesus Christ commanded to all nations.
Seek forgiveness for iniquities by offering a scapegoat laden with the sins of Israel, despatching it into the wilderness.	Forgive sins in the name of Jesus Christ, by the delegated power of Christ.
Pray for the People.	Pray for the people.

THE MASS

The Exodus theme represents the central fact of Israel's history. The Exodus event is to the Jewish people what the Christ event is to Christians.

    a. It is the basis of Israel's faith. Redemption from Egypt and God making them His people.

    b. It is the basis of Israel's hope.

The Exodus event holds the central position in Israel's liturgy.

The whole purpose of the Passover celebration (the Seder) was to recall in thankfulness the saving works of the first Exodus, and stir up hope in a greater deliverance yet to come.

Most significantly, Jesus chose the Passover meal, the sacramental memorial of the Israelites' Exodus from Egypt, as the sacramental memorial of His passage, or exodus, of His humanity from its fallen condition due to sin, to its transfigured life in God. In the institution of the Eucharist, Jesus linked the central event of the New Testament — His passion, death and resurrection — with the central event of the Old Testament, the passover from slavery in Egypt to the freedom of the promised land.

From the New Testament scriptures we know that Jesus looked at His life's work and mission in terms of the Old Testament. Several Exodus events are very important for Jews. The New Testament evangelists under the inspiration of the Holy Spirit gave these same events a deeper spiritual meaning. I want to compare some of these actual Old Testament events to their deeper meaning, given in New Testament writings.

1.   In the Exodus event we see how God sent Moses to deliver the people of Israel from slavery in Egypt by working miracles and bringing them to the promised land. From the New Testament we know that God sent His Son Jesus to free us from the slavery of sin and by His death God performed the greatest of all miracles, Jesus's resurrection, thereby opening Heaven for us (Romans 5:12-21, 6:20-23, Hebrews 10:12).

2.   During the Exodus, God miraculously fed Israel in the desert with manna (Exodus 16:4-5,31-35). Jesus gives us His body, the Eucharist, which is the Bread of Life (John 6).

3. God establishes the Jewish priesthood with Aaron and his descendants (Exodus 28,29). At the Last Supper, Jesus established a new priesthood not based on genealogy (Matthew 16:18-19).

4. In the desert God made a covenant with Israel sealed in the blood of lambs (Exodus 24:7-8). Jesus at the Last Supper made a new and everlasting covenant with us and sealed it in His own blood (Luke 22:20).

5. God orders the remembrance of the Exodus by celebrating each year the feast of the Passover (Exodus 12:21-28,13:9,10). At the Last Supper Jesus said, "Do this in remembrance of me" by celebrating the Eucharist (Luke 22:19).

All this leads to rituals that express God's saving actions and our hope for things to come. Hence we have the Seder for Jews and the Mass for Christians. The Passover (Seder) celebration has three main elements: (1) a memorial, (2) renewal of the covenant, and (3) hope of the final consummation. These same elements comprise the Eucharistic celebration, the Mass.

1. **Memorial** - The Passover celebration reminds Jews of God's acts and what He did for them, i.e., freed them from slavery, brought them to the promised land, and made Israel His own people (Deuteronomy 26:5-9). It is expressed in symbols of lamb (Exodus 12:5-6,27), unleavened bread (Exodus 12:39), and bitter herbs (Exodus 1:14). The Mass is a memorial of Christ's passion, death, and resurrection. It reminds us that Jesus died for all people so that we can reach the promised land, heaven, and have eternal life (1 Corinthians 11:26).

2. **Renewal of the Covenant** - Through the eating of the Seder meal Jews today (and in all generations) are linked with their forefathers in the Exodus. From the Seder liturgy we read the following:

> **In every generation each individual is bound to regard himself as if he had gone personally forth from Egypt. Therefore, we are bound to thank, praise, laud, glorify, extol, honor, bless, exalt and reverence Him who per-**

> formed for our fathers, and for us all these miracles. He
> brought us from slavery to freedom, from sorrow to joy,
> from mourning to festivity and from servitude to redemp-
> tion. Let us therefore sing a new song in His presence.
> Hallelujah.

The Eucharist is the renewal of the new covenant because
as a sacrament it unites us to Christ especially through the
meal, Holy Communion, i.e., the eating of the true Bread of
Life, the Body of our Lord. One might ask whether the Eucharist would have this power to unite us to Jesus in this
manner if it were only a "symbol" of our Lord.

3. **Hope of the Final Consummation** - The Seder expresses
   Israel's hope and faith for the fulfillment in the coming of
   the messiah and resurrection of the dead. The Eucharist is
   the pledge of the final consummation and anticipation of
   the heavenly banquet (Luke 22:14-18).

The Mass is not some act the Church instituted because it is a
nice way or a mysterious way or even a holy way to worship God.
The seeds of the Mass were planted in the desert journey of the Jews
more than 3,000 years ago when God made Israel His people via a
covenant. The Mass became reality on the night our Lord celebrated
the Last Supper, i.e., when He replaced the passover of the Old Testament with the passover of the New Testament (which was His
passing from death to life).

The Seder and the Mass have similar essential parts. The Seder
has three components: the Haggadah, or telling about God's wonderful work; the blessing, thanksgiving, the grace at the meal; and
the actual redoing of the saving event, or eating of the meal. And
here is the Christian Mass in its most essential parts: Liturgy of the
Word; the narrative of God's words and deeds; Liturgy of the Eucharist: our grateful response of thanksgiving which sacramentally re-
enacts those saving deeds, thus making us a part of them, making
those same saving deeds vitally our own. Continuing the distin-
guishing characteristic Judaic worship, the congregation, after being confronted anew with God's mighty saving actions, engages in
the sacrificial meal, Holy Communion.

The favorite symbol in rabbinic literature to describe the messianic kingdom was that of a banquet. Christ gave an unexpected deep-
ening to the rabbinic image; the messianic meal was a paschal meal.

The Eucharist is the earthly sacramental anticipation of the feast to be celebrated in the Kingdom of Heaven, and the heavenly banquet is a prolongation of the Eucharist supper. Christ in fulfilling the Pasch inaugurated His Kingdom in which His followers could already share by eating of His paschal Body and Blood and receive in Christ, God's glorifying action.

CHRIST'S REAL PRESENCE IN THE EUCHARIST

In the original Temple of Jerusalem (Solomon's Temple; c. 950 B.C.) stood an innermost sanctuary or back room (Debir), later called the Holy of Holies. This back room was the proper abode of Yahweh, housing also His throne, i.e., the Ark of the Covenant. According to Deuteronomy 10:1-5, Moses built an ark of acacia wood at Yahweh's command, and put inside it the two stone tablets on which Yahweh had written the Ten Commandments. Besides the Ark, the Debir contained two large gilded wooden figures called cherubim, whose outstretched wings protected the Ark and were thought to afford a throne for God, Who, of course, was not represented by any figure. A veil separated the Holy of Holies from other sections of the Temple. It was believed Yahweh was enthroned above the Ark and the Cherubim in a thick cloud (1 Kings 8:1-13). This belief in Yahweh's presence in His Temple was the whole reason for the worship celebrated there and for the pious customs of the faithful. Solomon's Temple was destroyed around 586 B.C. Also, at this time the Ark of the Covenant disappeared or was destroyed. After the Babylonian exile, a more modest Temple (called the Zorobabel) was built (515 B.C.) according to the pattern and on the site of the former Temple (Ezra 1,3,6). This Temple was plundered and desecrated in 169 B.C. by Antiochus IV Epiphanes (1 Maccabees 1:21-26, 2 Maccabees 5:15-21). In 19 B.C. Herod the Great undertook reconstruction of the Temple, and completed the essential structure in about 10 years. Like the Zorababel Temple, a veil separated the Holy of Holies from the other sanctuaries, which was torn in two by Jesus' death (Matthew 27:51). After the destruction of the Temple by the Romans in 71 A.D. and the disappearance of the Levitical priesthood, Jewish worship centered around the Torah in the synagogue. (See heading in Chapter 2, on the Synagogue).

Throughout the centuries many Christians have questioned the divinity of Christ. Most Protestants and many Catholics do not believe in the Real Presence of Jesus in the Eucharist. The Jews murmured when our Lord told them that He would give them the bread of eternal salvation, His Flesh to eat and His Blood to drink. They found it hard to lift their minds up to a proper understanding of their history as the chosen children of God. Christ reminded them:

> **Your fathers ate the manna in the desert and they are dead...the bread that I shall give is My Flesh for the life of the world.** (John 6:49-51)

Surely they understood, better than many Christians do today, that what Christ said was to be taken literally, for,

> **The Jews on that account argued with one another, saying: How can this man give us His Flesh to eat?** (John 6:52)

Skeptics, like the Jews of Christ's day, look at the material aspects of things for the basis of human understanding, not back to the supernatural source, nor forward to their supernatural destiny. Consequently, they fail to grasp the essence of things, putting all their faith in that which perishes. Christ did not say to the doubting Jews, what Protestants say, that by **"This is My Body"** He meant that **"This represents My body."** No, He solemnly insisted upon conditions which made plain that His actual Flesh and Blood must be eaten for salvation.

> **Jesus replied: 'I tell you most solemnly, if you do not eat the Flesh of the Son of Man and drink His Blood, you will not have life in you. Anyone who does eat My Flesh and drink My Blood has eternal life, and I shall raise him up on the last day. For My Flesh is real food and My Blood is real drink. He who eats My Flesh and drinks My Blood lives in Me and I live in him.'** (John 6:53-56)

John tells us that Jesus taught this doctrine in the Synagogue at Capernaum. And His followers had a tough time accepting that,

> **After this, many of His disciples left Him and stopped going with Him.** (John 6:59-66)

Again, would the disciples have left Him if they thought Jesus was only speaking symbolically?

All Catholic churches have a Tabernacle which houses the Blessed Sacrament. Near the Tabernacle a Sanctuary lamp burns continuously as a sign of the Real Presence of Christ. How blessed Catholics are. Men, women, or children can approach God in the

Tabernacle and pray in His presence. In the days of the Temple of Jerusalem only the High Priest could enter the Holy of Holies and then only once a year on the Day of Atonement. Yet, how many Catholics make use of this Divine gift from our Lord?

CONFESSION

I first learned about Confession from Catholic friends in high school and college. It seemed that they could commit sins all week long, go to Confession on Saturday, and start sinning again until they went to Confession the following Saturday. My Protestant friends had this same view regarding Catholics and Confession. Being a Jew at the time, I thought this behavior ridiculous. How can someone sin, go confess to a man (priest) and then go right back to doing the same thing again time after time? It did not make sense one reconciles with God in this manner. Asking God forgiveness should include the intention of trying to change one's ways and the desire to follow His laws. It was not until I went through my conversion process that I first learned what the Sacrament of Penance (Confession) meant. Then I realized what a misconception many Catholics and Protestants had regarding the correct teaching of the Catholic Church concerning this sacrament. Many Catholics believe they do not need an intermediary, or priest, and can go directly to God for the forgiveness of their sins. They see sin and forgiveness as a private matter between themselves and God and only God can forgive their sins. Many do not believe or know that when one sins seriously against God one also sins against the community of believers, the Church, and needs to be reconciled with that community as well. Although as a Jew I believed that only God could forgive sins, I came to realize, as taught by the Gospels and the Church, that Jesus did indeed delegate to sinful men the power to forgive sins.

Because Jews believed only God could forgive sins, the Scribes were furious with Jesus and called Him a blasphemer when He cured a paralytic with the words, "**Courage, my child, your sins are forgiven**" (Matthew 9:1-8). They would rather accuse Jesus of performing sorcery with the help of the devil than believe that He had the authority and power to forgive sin. They couldn't accept the fact that God would give the power to forgive sin to man. The Scribes considered Jesus only a man, not God.

Jesus specifically gave the power to forgive sin to men when He said,

> You are Peter and on this rock I will build my Church, and the
> gates of the underworld can never hold out against it. I will give
> you the Keys of the Kingdom of Heaven, whatever you bind on
> earth shall be considered bound in Heaven; whatever you loose on
> earth shall be considered loosed in Heaven. (Matthew 16:18-19)

And in John's Gospel,

> 'As the Father sent Me so am I sending you.' After saying this He
> breathed on them and said: 'Receive the Holy Spirit. For those
> whose sins you forgive, they are forgiven; for those whose sins
> you retain, they are retained. (John 20:21-23)

The New Testament clearly states, then, that God gave the Apostles
the power not only to forgive sin but also to retain sin.

During my conversion process I read in various Protestant writings that the power to forgive sins was meant only for the Apostles
and was not passed on to their successors (Bishops) as taught by the
Catholic Church. This made no sense. Why would Jesus place such
a big obstacle before potential Jewish converts if this power would
last only for the relatively short life span of a few Apostles? If Jesus
gave this great power to the Apostles He must have done so because
it would be of great benefit to the Church. And if were needed by
the Church at its very beginning, why would it not be needed during all the ages the Church awaited our Lord's return? Is the Church
today not the same Church founded on the Rock Peter, to whom the
"Keys" were given for our benefit as well?

Although the Divine institution and the particular confession
of sins as a necessity for salvation is not explicitly expressed in
Scripture, it is a necessary consequence of the judicial power to
forgive sins. The power of remitting sins or retaining them can only
be properly exercised if the possessor of the power of penance knows
both the sins and the disposition of the penitent. In the fourteenth
session of the Council of Trent on March 25,1551, the doctrine of
penance was set down in great detail because of repeated attacks on
this sacrament by the Reformers during the Protestant Reformation.
The following are excerpts from that document:

> The universal Church has always understood that integral con-
> fession of sins was likewise prescribed by our Lord (see James
> 5:16;1 John 1:9; Luke 17:14), and that by divine law this integral
> confession is necessary for all those who have fallen after bap-
> tism. For our Lord Jesus Christ, as He was about to ascend from

earm to heaven, lett prIests to be t1is vicars (Matthew 16:19; 18:18; John 20:23), as rulers and judges to whose authority Christians are to submit all mortal sins that they have fallen into. In accordance with the power of the keys, the priests are to pronounce sentence of forgiveness or retention of sins. Now it is clear that if priests did not know the case, they could not exercise this judgement, nor could they observe equity in imposing penances if the penitents declared their sins in a general way only, instead of specifically and particularly... Further, it is wicked to call confession a torturing of consciences. For it is clear that all the Church demands of each penitent is that he examine himself rather carefully and look into the innermost recesses of his conscience, and that he confess those sins by which he remembers having mortally offended his Lord and God... The difficulty and the shame of confessing one's sins could seem heavy indeed, if it were not lightened by many wonderful advantages and consolations which most assuredly are conferred in absolution on all those who approach this sacrament worthily.

The Sacrament of Penance (Confession) has undergone a long development in the Church from the time Jesus gave the power to forgive and retain sin to the Apostles, to its present form. This development has been guided by the Holy Spirit and entrusted by our Lord to the Catholic Church.

IMAGES, STATUES AND ICONS

In the Ten Commandments God gave to Moses on Sinai we read the following:

You shall not make yourself a carved image or any likeness of anything in heaven or on earth beneath or in the waters under the earth; you shall not bow down to them or serve them. (Exodus 20 :4)

As a Jew I felt that statues and icons in churches were forms of idol worship and a violation of the Ten Commandments. Many Protestant Christians also feel that way. As I was going through my conversion process to Christ, I realized (with the Church's help) that God referred to images considered equal to Him that man worshiped as gods. In the Catholic and Orthodox Churches statues and icons of Jesus and saints are not worshiped or adored. Catholics do not have to worship a statue of Jesus when they have the real Christ in the Eucharist. Statues of saints help us to prayerfully reflect on the lives of the saints who followed God's law faithfully, thereby reminding us to do the same.

SALVATION OUTSIDETHE CHURCH

The section on Immortality in chapter 2 mentions, for the most part, that the Talmud offers little assurance of a blissful immortality to anyone but Jews. What does Christianity say about who can be saved and achieve eternal bliss with God?

> **The Church teaches that: God wills the salvation of all men; men are saved in and through Christ; membership in the Church established by Christ, known and understood as the community of salvation, is necessary for salvation; men with this knowledge and understanding who deliberately reject this Church, cannot be saved. The Catholic Church is the Church founded by Christ.**
> (Catholic Almanac 1990)

Does this mean we have to believe in Jesus and be baptized to be saved? What about those who never heard of Christ or who in good conscience are not convinced He is their Savior? Can an atheist be saved? Many Protestant Churches, especially Fundamentalist churches, teach that only baptized-Christians can be saved. I had a big problem with this type of thinking since it meant my mother, a good person who believed in God and was responsible for my deep faith, could not get to Heaven because she did not believe in Christ. Happily I learned what the Catholic Church teaches regarding this matter. The Second Vatican Council, which was in session during my conversion process, covered this subject summarily in the following manner:

> **Those also can attain to everlasting salvation who through no fault of their own do not know the Gospel of Christ or his Church, yet sincerely seek God and, moved by grace, strive by their deeds to do his will as it is known to them through the dictates of conscience. Nor does divine Providence deny the help necessary for salvation to those who, without blame on their part, have not yet arrived at an explicit knowledge of God, but who strive to live a good life, thanks to his grace. Whatever good or truth is found among them is looked upon by the Church as a preparation for the Gospel. She regards such qualities as given by him who enlightens all men so that they may finally have life.** (Dogmatic Constitution on the Church, No. 16)

THE BLESSED VIRGIN MARY

The Blessed Virgin Mary is the greatest human being ever created.

In the play and movie "Fiddler on the Roof," a poignant scene takes place on a Friday eve as the father, Tevye, and his wife lead the family circle in a tender Sabbath prayer. Tevye desires his daughters to grow up learned in the ways of the Bible. He prays that they "may be like Ruth and Esther; that they too may be deserving of praise." But Ruth and Esther are not the only great Jewish women of the Old Testament. There are also Sara, Rebecca, Rachel, Deborah, and Judith. Traditional Judaism reveres and praises these women of ancient Israel. Every child learns very early who they are and what importance they hold in the faith.

In such an atmosphere of devotion I grew up. And yet, there was a time when I belittled and made fun of the greatest Woman in all Scripture, Mary, the Mother of God. I couldn't see why Catholics put Her on a high pedestal. They pray to Her, light candles at Her statues, and ask Her for favors. It looked to me like idol worship. I could not comprehend it. Of course, at that time I didn't believe in Christ either. Once I received the gift of faith in Jesus, I took another look at my attitude towards Mary. If all my life I had been taught to honor and praise the great Jewish women of the Old Testament, then should I not honor and praise the Jewish Woman Who gave to the world the Son of God?

I found the answer in St. John's Gospel. While our Lord was dying on the cross, He pronounced the following:

Seeing His Mother there with the disciple whom He loved, Jesus said to His Mother, 'Woman, there is Your son'. In turn He said to the disciple, 'There is your Mother.' (John 19:26-27)

At such a moment Jesus was not concerned about who would take care of His Mother. Such arrangements would have been made much earlier. The statement conveyed a "sign" of the spiritual Motherhood of Mary, the new Eve and Mother of the faithful and indeed all humanity. John is mystically the representative of the human race called to be spiritual children of Mary. This can be seen from Scripture and it is what the Catholic and Orthodox Churches have always believed.

The New Testament tells us that if we love, this is sufficient guarantee God lives and is active in us. In this life we come closer to

God through love than through knowledge. For me there is no greater example of this truth besides Jesus than Mary, a simple Jewish Mother who has greatly influenced my life. She was not a great theologian or philosopher or queen or political leader. She was simply the Mother of Jesus, Who obeyed the will of God without question. Mary's life and example is an integral part of the Good News. The last chapter of this book is devoted to Her.

In October 1962, after spending almost two years of reading, studying, and reflecting, on Jesus and the Catholic Church, I went to the rectory of the local parish church, Christ the King, in Commack, NY. Here I met Father Savastano. Armed with my new-found knowledge, I told him briefly of my background and desire to be baptized right away. Father told me that I would first have to receive instruction. Initially disappointed, I found the instruction period most helpful. Father and I got to know each other. A kind, compassionate, and humble priest, he was devoting his life to Jesus and the Church. At the end of the instruction period he told me how much he appreciated my telling him about my Jewish background and beliefs, and how they had been instrumental in leading me to Jesus and the Catholic Church.

During my instruction period on January 19, 1963, Irma gave birth to a girl born prematurely at seven months. The baby weighed only two pounds, had no neck, and died after seven hours. We named her Lisa and buried her in a Jewish cemetery. Several years later I found out that a nurse had quietly baptized Lisa before her death.

On February 23, 1963, Father Savastano baptized me and my son Stephen, now five. At my baptism I took the name Paul, in honor of St. Paul, who had become sort of a mentor to me during my conversion process. The next day I received my First Holy Communion. These were two great days in my life!

In Sinai, God elevated Israel by making the Israelites His Chosen People. This election was orientated towards the coming of the Messiah. Before He came the calling heralded His coming. Pentecost, a Jewish feast commemorating the gift of the Law to Israel on Mt. Sinai, represented the beginning of the new Chosen People, the Church, by the coming of the Holy Spirit. This election is by grace, and since He came, it is to witness to His coming and the salvation He has brought. St. Paul poses the following question about the Jews:

> **Let me put a further question then: is it possible that God has rejected his people? Of course not. I, an Israelite, descended from Abraham through the tribe of Benjamin, could never agree that God had rejected his people, the people he chose especially long ago.** (Romans 11:1-2)

God never takes back His gifts or revokes his choice. Therefore Israel remains the chosen people and this call has not been revoked but continues. I will be eternally grateful to God for being **"twice chosen"**: first, to begin my life as part of the Old Israel and, secondly, to end my life as part of the New Israel.

Within a few months after my baptism, Irma started taking instruction with Father Savastano. She received the Sacrament of Baptism October 19,1963. Soon afterwards we both received the Sacrament of Confirmation. For my Confirmation, I took the name Joseph. Since I was raised without a father, St. Joseph, from then on, would be my father, as Mary was my Mother.

A few words regarding St. Joseph seem appropriate here. In Judaism it is the father, not the mother, who plays a significant role as a boy goes through the Jewish rites of circumcision, redemption, and Bar Mitzvah. The father also assumes important duties by participating with his son in the synagogue worship services. Little is written in the scriptures about St. Joseph. Yet St. Joseph, as the "foster" father of Jesus, played an important part in the Jewish rites undergone by Jesus, including the participation with Jesus in the worship services in the synagogue and Temple as He grew up. I believe it is important and fitting that all Christians honor St. Joseph, who willingly assumed his responsibilities as the "father" of Jesus and the husband of Mary. He was head of the Holy Family.

Months before my baptism I prayed intensely to Jesus and Mary that my mother would not be devastated by my conversion. After all, it was she who made me practice the Jewish faith. I had been the only one in my family that could pray in Hebrew and lead the Sabbath worship services as a cantor in the synagogue I attended years earlier. She was very proud of that. After Irma and I told her we had become Catholic, her reaction surprised us. Quite simply she told us we were nuts but she still loved us and her grandson.

I had neglected however to pray for Irma's parents. I thought because they were basically agnostic they wouldn't care about our conversion. I was wrong. Her father never talked to us again and would not even acknowledge his grandson whom he loved deeply. Irma's mother kept in touch with us, saw us occasionally, and of course blamed me for the break in our family.

CHAPTER 5
THE CATHOLIC YEARS

After my baptism I began attending daily Mass, saying the Rosary each day, and going frequently to confession. I joined the Perpetual Adoration Society and the Holy Name Society. On First Fridays I would spend one hour in prayer before the Blessed Sacrament.

In 1963 Irma became pregnant again. During her pregnancy she developed an extremely high blood-sugar level which necessitated that she spend five days in the hospital to stabilize her condition. On March 9, 1964, our daughter Andrea Patrice was born by C-section, weighing almost 10 pounds. Everything appeared normal. Happily I phoned Father Savastano with the good news. Although he was very busy that day, he promised to visit them both the next day. That afternoon I received a telephone call from our pediatrician expressing concern about the baby's condition. Her lungs were filling with fluid. This same malady afflicted President and Mrs. Kennedy's new-born son Patrick who died in 1963. I immediately called Father Savastano; he already knew. Earlier in the day something had prompted him to visit the hospital and upon seeing Andrea baptized her.

In the evening I returned to the hospital to visit Irma and Andrea. The nurse let me see my baby who was in an incubator in the nursery. I told Irma the baby had developed a medical problem.

After spending some time with Irma, I went back to check on Andrea. When I got to the nursery all the blinds were drawn. I asked someone why the shades were down and was told a baby had just died. No one had to tell me it was Andrea. I checked and learned it indeed was Andrea. This time I could not fake it. I immediately told Irma the sad news. I do not believe it's necessary to describe what happened then or how we felt. Two days later Father said a Mass of Angels for Andrea. Except for a friend, Frank, who didn't want me to be alone and the baby in the little white coffin, nobody else attended the Mass. Irma remained in the hospital. After the service, Father and I took Andrea to the cemetery and buried her.

I cannot explain the mystery of why the Lord takes children from those who want them and allows others who don't want them to have them. But it is no mystery that God is a God of Love. Three times now God took to Himself our children.

My faith in the Lord helped me understand that God knew what He was doing. Some day He will show each of us why trusting in Him during all the pain and suffering we experienced on earth was necessary and ultimately rewarding.

My father-in-law never called or came to see his daughter. My mother-in-law came to the hospital to see Irma on the day of the baby's burial and then stayed overnight at my home. That evening while we sat alone in the kitchen, Irma's mother told me about her problems and that my actions had split the family. She was trying to justify her husband's behavior. Near the end of our conversation I went into the bedroom, got a crucifix, and put it on the table in front of her. I proceeded to tell her she ought to kiss that figure on the cross. It was because of Him that no matter what she or her husband would ever say or do to me, they would always be welcomed in my house and be treated with the utmost respect. And, although they may hate me, they would remain in my prayers. I always prayed for reconciliation. It was their choice that it never happened. To this day, my father-in-law has not wanted to see my daughter or son. Yes, I still pray for him.

On March 1, 1965, Irma gave birth to another girl, Andrea Faith. This time there was no problem. Later that month Andrea was baptized. My mother even came to the Church for the baptism. Irma asked her later if she felt funny attending the ceremony. She responded, "Why should I feel funny? Isn't this God's house?" Yet some Catholics today are not sure whether a Catholic church is God's house.

In 1964 the thought came to me to study theology and possibly teach. I entered St. John's University in Jamaica, NY, to pursue a Master's degree in Theology. For three years I attended St. John's at night and graduated in June 1967. Unfortunately, the low pay theology teachers earned would have meant taking a drastic cut in salary. Irma was not prepared to do that. I need to point out that Irma's faith was not at the same level of intensity as mine. She had been brought up as a marginal Jew with little knowledge of Judaism. Religion never encompassed a big part of her life as it had mine. Although she came to believe in Christ, she was not very comfortable with some of the devotions fostered by the Church. She also had a tough time with the Sacrament of Confession. She did have a strong devotion to Mary's mother, St. Anne. Irma would always go to Mass on Sundays and Holy days, and would only miss Mass if she were sick. She was a good wife and mother and was always willing to help people in need.

In 1968 I went to work for a defense contractor in College Park, MD and we moved to Wheaton, MD. In 1970 I entered the Permanent Diaconate program run by the Washington Archdiocese. I entered government service in 1972 by going to work for the Naval Research Laboratory as an electronics engineer. On September 30, 1972, Cardinal Patrick O'Boyle, Archbishop of Washington, ordained me as a deacon and assigned me to my parish, St. John the Baptist Church in Silver Spring, MD. St. John's was a very progressive parish. As a deacon I would preach once a month at several masses. I became involved in private instruction to converts, and also had a social ministry. This entailed working with a soup kitchen named "So Others Might Eat" (SOME) in Washington, DC, and the House of Ruth, a home for battered women. Both organizations were relatively new in 1973. Unfortunately, as I pursued social, teaching, and liturgical ministries, my prayer life suffered drastically. No more daily Mass. No more rosaries. I justified my actions by saying that my work and ministries were really prayer, and therefore there was little need for devotional or private prayer. Today, in retrospect, I ask myself rhetorically how far would I have gotten with Mother Teresa and her Sisters if I told them that their work with the poor replaces their obligation to an intensive prayer life. In a few years my lack of prayer life would have a devastating effect on my spirituality and in some instances, I would not consider my behavior worthy of the name Christian, certainly not Catholic.

From the time of my ordination in 1972 to 1988 I had gone from being a "conservative" Catholic to becoming a very "liberal" Catholic. Some of the views I held then included the following:

1. Birth control — Contraception was not wrong if Catholics in good conscience felt they had to practice it.
2. Abortion — Although personally against abortion for any reason for Catholics and Jews, I felt we must respect freedom of others to choose.
3. Married Clergy — This should be optional.
4. Women priests — Church should ordain women to the priesthood.
5. Divorce — Church needs to be more open and compassionate, allow divorce on certain grounds.
6. Mortal Sin — This occurs only when one turns away completely from God.

I felt comfortable with my views in these areas even though I knew they from main-line Church teachings. I hoped the Church would modify its teachings regarding these issues because I thought they were not part of infallibly defined doctrine and therefore open to change. In 1975 I left St. John the Baptist and was assigned to a more conservative parish, St. Andrew the Apostle in Silver Spring, MD. I looked at this assignment as an opportunity to help open conservative Catholics to a more "enlightened" view of Catholicism. My assignments at St. Andrew's, such as preaching, instructing converts, and social ministry, were similar to those I undertook at St. John's. Although I held the views expressed above, I also taught converts what the Church taught.

It was during the 1970s that I came in contact with such Catholic movements as the Charismatic Renewal and Cursillo. In 1976 I made a Cursillo, and found it to be a wonderful experience. It was a great method for 1) developing a personal relationship with Jesus and 2) becoming an evangelizer. I was active in Cursillo as a spiritual director until 1981. This may sound odd, but the only problem I had with Cursillo was a lack of devotion to Mary. Even at the height of my liberalism I retained a great closeness to Her. I enjoyed giving homilies on Mary. In the late 1970s I would pray asking Her when She would return and tell us what we needed to do now, as She had done at Fatima. After all, the world desperately needed help. In 1978, John Paul II became Pope. This distressed me because I knew he would not support many of my liberal views. In fact, he stood on the opposite side of the spectrum from me on important issues for "modern" Catholics.

In 1975 a doctor diagnosed Irma as diabetic. In 1978 she began taking insulin shots, but she never really followed the doctor's direction. Sometime after 1978 Irma and I started drifting apart. Our marriage had become somewhat of a convenience. Little communication passed between us. Irma and I had practically become strangers. We hardly even shared our social ministry any more. Irma had worked hard in the parish helping the poor, especially Vietnamese families, to find homes, provide for their rent, and supply food. Originally a bundle of energy, she eventually relinquished her ministry as her health deteriorated. Our friends never knew that Irma and I had marital problems. Neither did our children. After all we never argued during this period. For me, Irma no longer seemed the same woman with whom I had fallen in love, and had been happily married for so many years. She had changed. I am not sure how she viewed me. Because of these problems I gave serious consideration to leaving the diaconate.

In December 1981 Irma formed a blood clot in her leg and was rushed to the hospital. The surgeon said she needed a simple surgical procedure that would take less than an hour. I sat in the waiting room for five hours until the surgeon finally came back. He told me Irma had a vascular system of a 75-year-old. He did not hold out much hope that she would live long.

Irma stayed in the hospital four months. During that time she became practically blind, one leg was amputated, and her kidneys and liver barely functioned. By March 1982 she was barely lucid. During this period I prayed constantly for her. I asked the Lord why it was not I who was suffering in that bed instead of her. For four months I visited her almost every night watching her deteriorate. She taught me a lot about dying. I hope that when my time comes I can be as courageous as she was.

In our years at St. Andrew's Irma and I had become very friendly with Father Anthony DeVial. Father Anthony, a priest from France, worked on a lay family program and was assigned to our Church. He saw Irma frequently during her hospitalization and gave her the sacraments of Anointing of the Sick and Confession. In one of her lucid moments she told Father Anthony that when she got to heaven she would tell Jesus to send Charlie a good wife because he deserved one. Irma knew that as a deacon I could never remarry. She did not like that rule. She expected me to remarry. If I did not, it meant to her, that our marriage did not mean much to me. On March 30,1982, Irma died peacefully and went to her reward. During her illness she never said, "Why me God," even though she knew she was dying. Several hundred people attended her wake in spite of a very rainy night. On April 1, after a beautiful Mass, concelebrated by many priests, she was laid to rest in Gate of Heaven Cemetery in Wheaton, MD.

I would be remiss if I didn't mention Irma's friend Jean. Irma met her on a Cursillo weekend in 1976. Jean, who also was a Jewish convert to Catholicism, became a close friend to Irma. She went to the hospital many times while I was at work. Jean was the friend that Irma desperately needed to confide in especially during the period when little communication passed between us. I will always be grateful to Jean for being a good friend to Irma.

One of my cousins, who happens to be a doctor, told me after Irma's death that diabetes not treated properly, can change a person's personality, and I should not blame myself for marital problems we had during the latter stages of her illness. Yet I still feel sad at my insensitivity towards Irma during that period. Feeling sorry for myself, I did not comprehend the pain she was under going. It is obvious to me now, that I was not the "model" deacon many believed me to be. Looking back on the period of Irma's illness and after her death, I can now see clearly to what depths I had sunk because I neglected prayer.

After a tragedy occurs in one's life, a person can sink into a form of isolation especially if one is spiritually bankrupt or depressed. That happened to me. After Irma's death only a few people called to inquire how I felt. None of my priest or deacon acquaintances, except for Father DeVial, checked on me. Their lack of concern bothered me. However, it was partly my fault because I was not always accessible either. For instance, there were Fran and Nick who called frequently inviting me to their house for dinner. I always seemed to have some excuse for not going. Others included Bob and Sue, friends from Cursillo, who came over to my house just to be with me. I could freely confide in Bob and Sue since we shared common views on a lot of things, especially the Church. To them, I will always be thankful for being there. I did receive a lot of support during Irma's illness and after her death from associates in the Navy. In particular, PV, a Navy Captain for whom I worked at the time, was especially supportive and a good friend. Despite such strong friendships, I felt sorry for myself and very lonely. I yearned for female companionship so I started dating. I took a self-imposed leave from all diaconate functions. I decided not to remain celibate and would remarry when the right woman came along. One evening while sitting in my living room I began to cry and pray. This life-style of dating disturbed me, so I asked God to send me someone good. He answered my prayer shortly.

Before relating what happened next I need to explain a chance meeting that took place a week before Irma died. My daughter Andrea and I had gone to dinner at a restaurant with some friends. After dinner Andrea walked over to the square shaped bar and started talking to a young fellow standing there. Since she was under a lot of stress, I decided to wait at the opposite side of the bar and let her talk. Some women stood at the bar next to me waiting for a table. I began a conversation with one of them (her name was Pilar) and learned that she worked for the National Conference of Catholic Bishops. I told Pilar I was a deacon in the Catholic Church and that I was at the bar keeping an eye on my daughter. I also told her about my wife's illness and her impending death. During our conversation she asked whether I would consider remarriage some day, and I replied "maybe". She said if the time came that I would like to meet some one special, she had a wonderful friend and co-worker named Sara whom she would like me to meet. I told her that possibly in the future I would like to meet her since she sounded like a wonderful person. I gave Pilar my work phone number because she wanted to check on us and some day introduce me to her friend. Then, I motioned to Andrea that we had to go home. Irma died the following Monday.

When Pilar told Sara that she had met a nice man at a bar and wanted us to meet, Sara declined. She thought what kind of man, who claims to be a deacon, takes his daughter to a bar while his wife is dying in the hospital. At Mass the Sunday following Irma's death, Pilar heard, during the prayer of the faithful, that deacon Charles Hoffman's wife had died. Pilar told Sara the news she had heard at Church. Finally, after a time and due to her persistence, Sara allowed Pilar to give me her phone number at work only. It was Pilar who happened to call me shortly after I prayed in the living room. She had told me again about Sara and encouraged me to call her. A few days later I did call Sara. We talked for almost thirty minutes, mostly about the Church. I felt so good talking to her that I asked her for a date. Sara lived only about ten minutes from my house. One evening I drove over to Sara's house and met her. When I arrived I met also her three teenage sons, Donald, Mark and Eric as well as her parents and her brother, all of whom lived with her. Normally a man going on his first date with a woman would have been overwhelmed to meet all these people. But I was not; I will explain why later. Sara and I went to a nearby place for a drink and spent over two hours talking. For the first time in a long while, I enjoyed being with someone and being able to freely and easily communicate with her. Sara and I enjoyed our first date and we started seeing each other often. It was not long before I decided this was the woman I wanted to marry.

I would like to say a few words about Sara's background. Sara was born in Lima, Peru, November 21,1942. Her paternal grandfather was a Jew who migrated to Peru from Turkey at the turn of the twentieth century. Sara received her education in a Catholic school run by the Sisters of the Immaculate Heart of Mary from Philadelphia, PA. Throughout high school all her classes were taught in English and Spanish. After graduating from high school Sara came to the United States in October 1962 to study medicine. While working with paraplegic veterans she met her first husband who came frequently to visit his uncle, a paraplegic. They started dating and in September 1963 were married. They had three sons. Sara's upbringing taught her that a woman must be a faithful wife, a good mother, and she must serve her husband. By 1967, her husband had become very abusive to her, unfaithful to his marriage vows, and, in general very irresponsible. He was a nonpracticing Catholic, even before his marriage to Sara, with almost no knowledge of the Catholic faith. He possessed no understanding of Catholic teaching regarding marriage. In desperation, Sara tried to find the priest who married them. Unfortunately the priest had left the church and had married. Next she went to one of the parishes in Los Angeles seeking help. At the rectory she met a priest and told him her problem, but his response was cold and blunt. At the time she needed a priest with compassion who could advise her. The priest told her that since she married in the Catholic Church she must carry her cross. Sara wondered how he could say this to her since he personally did not know her difficult situation. In fact, he did not even seem to care. Leaving the rectory devastated, Sara walked away from the Church and in fact stayed away from the Sacraments many years. In 1968 Sara divorced her husband. In 1972 she went back to Peru with her sons to live with her parents and work with the Peace Corps. While in Peru she met an understanding priest. He was able to bring her back to the Church and to the Sacraments.

In 1976 Sara returned to the United States and settled in Washington, DC. After first working for a defense consulting firm, she found employment in 1978 with the National Conference of Catholic Bishops in the office for Hispanic Affairs. In 1979 her parents and youngest brother Ricardo came to this country to live with her. Sara wanted her family here with her because she never planned to remarry. Sara's other brother lives in Peru with his family. Difficult years followed. She worked a second job in the evenings and translated documents at night to support her family. Another reason Sara had no intention of marrying was her commitment to care always for her youngest brother who is mentally handicapped and unable to support himself or live alone. What attracted me most to Sara, besides her looks and bubbling personality, was her love for her family and the struggles she endured to keep them together. Her steadfastness in raising her children can serve as an inspiration to many single mothers today facing similar hardships.

Once Sara and I decided to marry, I requested a dispensation to marry and Sara applied for an annulment. It is necessary to point out one of the regulations permanent deacons are obliged to follow after the death of a wife. Pope Paul VI issued on his own initiative June 18,1967, a document entitled "Sacred Order of the Diaconate." One of the requirements in the document stated, "Qualified married men over 35 years of age or older may be ordained permanent deacons. The consent of the wife of a prospective deacon is required. A married deacon cannot remarry after the death of his wife." During the diaconate training program (1970-1972) leading to ordination, we were told that the Church, in its up coming revision of the Code of Canon Law, would very likely permit permanent deacons to remarry after the death of a wife. At the time of my ordination, as well as before and after, I never took a vow or made a promise to remain celibate if my wife should die. Only those men who were single at the time of ordination took a vow of celibacy. The new Code of Canon Law did not have the changes we expected.

After I submitted my request for dispensation from celibacy or laicization, I received a letter from the Archdiocese which recommended I go on a retreat to reflect whether or not marriage was the right decision for me. This response upset me since I considered myself a mature adult (48 year old) knowing quite well what a marriage commitment meant. Still being at a spiritual low and having no prayer life, additional letter exchanges with the Archdiocese upset me even more. Sara and I decided to get married civilly on August 13, 1982. By attempting marriage prior to my laicization I incurred an automatic suspension from the diaconate. After our marriage Sara and I continued attending Mass on Sundays and Holy Days. We also went to Communion. I knew about the church teaching of not going to Communion while living in the state of mortal sin. And in the eyes of the Church, Sara and I were living in mortal sin. Yet, in our "conscience" we felt nothing wrong with our receiving Communion because we didn't believe we were sinning. I also did not feel any need to go to Confession. In 1983 Sara moved to a new position at work. She became the office manager in the General Secretary's office and reported directly to Msgr. Hoye, the general secretary of the National Conference of Catholic Bishops. As office manager her main tasks included preparing for all annual bishops meetings, completing all the required documentation prior to the meetings and the minutes after the meetings, and supervising the support staff during the meetings. I usually worked as a volunteer during the bishops meetings and got to know some of the bishops.

Then in 1984 I started considering the possibility of leaving the Catholic Church and joining the Episcopal Church. The Episcopal Church would allow me to function as a deacon and maybe even become a priest some day. As a liberal Catholic, I felt in tune with many of the Episcopal Church's beliefs.

Two things kept me from leaving the Catholic Church. The first deterrent involved my devotion to the Blessed Mother. Which church, other than the Orthodox churches, has such devotion to Her as in the Catholic Church? I could never belong to any church where devotion to Mary was nonexistent or not fostered. The second reason may sound hypocritical considering I was a liberal Catholic. But maybe it illustrates a struggle within me that I was not really addressing. I came to the Catholic Church because I believed in the doctrine of infallibility of the Pope. Even though I disagreed with the Pope on several issues, for me, he was still Peter. He held all the authority Jesus gave to Peter. No other Christian church, except those in communion with Rome, accepted this doctrine. If I joined another church, I would be denying this doctrine. Without this doctrine, there could never be one true church as intended by Christ. There would be no guarantee that the Bible is the Word of God. And without an infallible church there could be no infallible witnessing to the fact that Jesus was truly God and that the One God is Triune consisting of three equal Divine Persons. So I stayed in the Catholic Church. Mary was surely watching over Sara and me.

During this unsettling period I received a call from a local priest, Father Mark. Father Mark, active in the Cursillo movement, noticed that I had gone to Communion at one of the Cursillo masses. At first, he was happy to see this because he thought that my marriage was now in order. He had called to verify this. When I told him the truth he proceeded to politely tell me that I was causing scandal when people who knew my situation saw Sara and me receiving Communion. This upset me and I proceeded to tell Father why I thought we were not doing anything wrong. The phone call from Father also upset Sara. After reflecting on my discussion with Father, I told Sara that it took a lot of courage for him to call. In fact he was the first priest to call me since Irma's funeral. I realized Father Mark had called because he was really concerned for us, as well as for other Catholics. Our actions could be influencing other Catholics in the wrong way. I came to respect him for what he did even though at the time I did not agree with him. In fact, in 1989 Father was to become my spiritual director and confessor for several years.

In 1984 I again requested dispensation, or laicization. Cardinal Hickey could not support my return to the diaconate ministry, but did support my request for laicization. In 1984 a rescript issued by the Congregation for the Sacraments included a dispensation from clerical celibacy and remission of the automatic suspension incurred by attempting marriage prior to laicization. Sara also received her annulment in 1984. On January 4, 1985 Sara and I were married in the Church during a beautiful Mass concelebrated by five priests with Father Anthony DeVial the main celebrant.

CHAPTER 6
THE SECOND CONVERSION

In 1987 I left government service and returned to private industry. That same year Sara was involved in preparing for the American Bishops' meeting with the Pope in September in Los Angeles, CA. Sara's boss, Msgr. Hoye, invited us to receive communion from the Pope during the Mass at Dodger Stadium. Here I was going to receive Holy Communion from the Vicar of Christ on earth. This was the same Pope I could not agree with on some important issues. We attended the Mass, and a few weeks later Sara received at her office two large photos of her and me receiving Communion from the Holy Father. I was quite moved. I believe now that was the beginning of another major conversion experience about to unfold in my life.

In 1986 my father-in-law Raphael, a man of 67, brilliant and kind, was diagnosed as having Alzheimer's disease. One month after the Pope's Mass in Los Angeles I happened to be watching the evening news on television with Raphael. I noticed he was talking to the TV. He was having a conversation with people on the screen. It brought tears to my eyes to see this. Raphael now lived in another world. I left the room and got out the volume for the Liturgy of the Hours appropriate for the season and began praying the evening prayer. This was the first time I prayed the hours since 1978. From that time on I would pray the hours once again each day.

In April 1988, a friend Elroy told me about a place called Medjugorje, Yugoslavia, where the Blessed Mother was allegedly appearing to six young visionaries each day since June 1981. He really believed in these apparitions. In June 1988, I started reading several books written by priests on the happenings in Medjugorje. What I read deeply moved me. Because of my theological background I was impressed with a book written by Dr. Mark Miravalle titled Heart of the Message of Medjugorje. Dr. Miravalle holds a doctorate degree in Sacred Theology from the Pontifical University of St. Thomas Acquinas, Rome and is an Associate Professor at the Franciscan University in Steubenville, OH. His doctoral dissertation topic was "The Message of Medjugorje in the Sources of Divine Revelation." His book looks at the messages of Mary and shows how very much in line they are with Scripture, Church council documents, and papal encyclicals.

Peace through faith, prayer, fasting, penance, and conversion summarizes the heart of Mary's message to the visionaries. This peace is not the peace the world gives, but as Jesus gives it (John 14:27). Mary says the greatest prayer is the Mass and She encourages daily attendance. She also tells the importance of monthly Confession, fasting on bread and water on Fridays if health and work permit, praying the Rosary daily, reading the Bible, devotion to the Blessed Sacrament, and respect to people of all faiths. Mary, maternally and compassionately, brings a message of love. Her messages contain no new revelation but support Catholic teachings.

Before studying the messages I first had to look at events taking place in Medjugorje to determine if they were true or fake. Being an engineer I decided first to read about the scientific investigations involving phenomena surrounding the visionaries. Although the scientific results were impressive they could never prove that the visionaries were indeed seeing what they claimed. Science can analyze the receiver (visionaries) as to whether they are hallucinating, in ecstacy, or even faking. But there is no way to analyze the transmitter, in this case, the Blessed Mother. Therefore, one must look at the fruits produced to see if what is occurring in Medjugorje is from God or a big lie fostered by Satan. Once again I was to use the same logic that brought me to recognize Jesus as my Lord and Savior. If the happenings in Medjugorje are not from God, things should have ended a long time ago. However, if our Blessed Mother is really appearing to these visionaries and giving them important messages for all of us, then these happenings would bear great fruits.

It has been said by some that the visionaries are lying, hallucinating, and are being manipulated by the Franciscan priests in Medjugorje. Having spent more than 30 years as an electronic engineer I found it impossible to believe that in this enlightened scientific age a group of very young people could sustain such a great deception for so long a period (since 1981). If they could, even guided by "priests," it would have had to be done with the help of Satan. But does Satan encourage people to go to daily Mass, pray the Rosary, go to monthly Confession, fast, promote family and group prayer? St. John tells us simply in his first letter:

> **It is not every spirit, my dear people, that you can trust; test them, to see they come from God; there are many false prophets, now, in the world. You can tell the spirits that come from God by this: every spirit which acknowledges that Jesus the Christ has come in the flesh is from God; but any spirit which will not say this of Jesus is not from God, but is the spirit of Antichrist, whose coming you were warned about.** (1 John 4:1-3)

Over the years, despite their fame, the visionaries have progressed into becoming very spiritual people, devoted to our Lord and His Mother and respectful of the Church and the hierarchy. The people of Medjugorje are the real miracle of the happenings there. No human power alone (and certainly not Satan) could have formed most of them into such a loving and peaceful worshipping community in such a short period of time.

Then we have the millions of pilgrims, young and old, who have come to Medjugorje since 1981. What makes them come to a place where there has been no "proof" of supernatural apparitions? More important, what makes them spend hours each day in prayer (Mass, the Rosary, Adoration), go to Confession and then return home and continue these practices including fasting? If the Blessed Mother was not behind all this in a unique way and the happenings (conversions) were not of supernatural origin, why then could not the devotion displayed in the parish of St. James be duplicated in every parish in the world? Surely, all Bishops and the Holy Father would welcome churches filled each day for hours with people praying, attending Mass and devotions, going to frequent Confession, and fasting. What a powerful witness this would be! Yet our churches are empty most of the time and locked even in the daytime for fear of vandalism. There are very few devotions if any in most parishes. Hardly any one goes to Confession anymore. Attendance at Mass is down.

I became convinced that the events in Medjugorje were real and had the support of God. By October 1988, motivated by messages of our Blessed Mother to the visionaries in Medjugorje, I had gone back to daily Mass, recited each day the Liturgy of Hours, went to monthly confession, prayed 15 decades of the Rosary daily, fasted on Fridays, and read scripture daily. I no longer had a problem with any of the Church's teachings as well as those expressed by our Holy Father and the hierarchy, had more awareness of and support for the poor, the homeless and the elderly, and began working on improving my ability to truly love and respect all people unconditionally.

Some people think of conversion normally as changing from one religion to another. Rarely do we think of conversion as changing from where we are now in our Catholic practices or attitudes (or lack thereof) to growing closer to God in our practices and attitudes. Because of the mercy and love of Jesus I have been able to experience both these types of conversion. The conversions in my life were supernatural because it was God who first enlightened me and then gave me the grace to accomplish the change. It was supernatural because in no way could I have changed on my own. And yes, I cannot prove the changes in me were of supernatural origin. It requires faith in God to understand the phenomenon of conversion.

For the second time in my life I experienced the peace of Christ. The Blessed Mother is right. This peace of Christ cannot be obtained through mere intellectual pursuit or by being inspired by great homilists, or even knowing the lives of saints. We can only achieve it through constant daily prayer and making the sacraments and devotions an integral part of our daily lives. It takes effort and work to achieve this peace. It cannot be handed to us on a silver platter. But there is nothing greater than to be and live in the peace of Christ. I can assure you that you will never have the need of a psychiatrist if you have this peace, no matter how disastrous the situation in which you may find yourself. It is a difficult task for those who have the peace, to share it with others. And share it we must. But it must be done lovingly, patiently and with humility, always respecting the other person and where he or she is in their relationship with God. But we do have the help of the Holy Spirit and our Mother Mary. As I was reading and learning about Medjugorje so was Sara. She too started going to daily Mass at work and praying the Rosary. Sara always had a deep devotion to our Blessed Mother. It is a blessing when spouses can share that devotion together.

Sara and I made our first pilgrimage to Medjugorje in November 1988. I went a second time in October 1989. Sara could not go because she was very busy preparing for the annual November Bishops' meeting in Washington, DC. We did go together again during Holy Week of 1990.

Our experiences in Medjugorje were always positive. The things that impressed us most were the town people, the clergy, and the visionaries. The people of Medjugorje are simple, relatively poor and loving people. I have never seen such devotion to Jesus, Mary, and the Church anywhere as exists there. Many of them, including the young people, spend hours in Church every evening attending the services. Young people formed prayer groups which meet very often to pray and share their faith. They are a courteous and humble people. The families with whom we stayed were beautiful. You could feel their devotion to Mary and the Lord and they went out of their way to serve us and make us comfortable. The Franciscan clergy in charge of the parish were and still are men of God clearly devoted to our Lord, His Mother, and the Church. They reflect the Gospel and Mary's message and are clearly committed to the teachings of Vatican Council II. They are not interested in material gain but in the salvation of souls. This is obvious from their lifestyles, preaching, and writings. My past experience in the Church has helped me tell the difference between priests devoted to authentic Church teachings and those who write their own agenda. The priests in Medjugorje are not working on their own agenda. The visionaries are basically simple and humble young people. They have not gained materially from their fame. There can be no doubt that our Blessed Mother was preparing the people of Medjugorje for sufferings they would have to endure due to the terrible war that started in 1992 with the break up of Yugoslavia.

I do not need physical proofs that the spiritual happening in Medjugorje is indeed a supernatural phenomenon. Faith relies not on physical proof. I cannot prove that the Resurrection of Jesus took place. I cannot prove that at Mass the bread and wine are transformed into the Body and Blood of our Lord Jesus Christ. I cannot prove the Assumption of our Blessed Mother into Heaven. There are many truths our Church teaches, even those not explicitly mentioned in the Bible, I cannot prove. Yet, I believe them all. The bishops of Yugoslavia issued a statement on the events in Medjugorje. On January 3,1991, the Catholic News Service (CNS) reported the following:

> In the statement drawn up Nov. 27-Z8,1992 [and passed onto the Vatican for review], the bishops [Yugoslav] recalled that the alleged apparitions, which began in 1981, have been the focus of studies at the diocesan and national level for several years. 'On the basis of research conducted so far, one cannot affirm that supernatural apparitions or revelation are involved,' the statement said. The continual flow of pilgrims to Medjugorje from various parts of the world, however, requires 'the attention and care of the bishops' it said. The statement suggested that the bishops conference work with the local bishop to set up pastoral and liturgical programs for the pilgrims, who make the trip 'motivated by faith'. In this way, it said, 'phenomena and contents that are not in agreement with the spirit of the church' can be avoided.

We must respect the Bishops' wishes and welcome their involvement in what happens in Medjugorje. They are concerned for our spiritual welfare and the credibility of the Church. We should be thankful to them. In time, I believe our Blessed Mother will provide the "physical" proof of the reality of Her apparitions in Medjugorje as She promised through the visionaries. I believe however, the real supernatural aspects of the happenings in Medjugorje are in the conversions that have taken place, first in the local people and then in the pilgrims — including Sara and me. However, the official judgement regarding the events in Medjugorje can only be made by the teaching authority of the Catholic Church (Magisterium). And I am ready to accept unconditionally the final judgement of the Church.

❖❖❖

In a very short period I went from a liberal Catholicism to what I would like to call, an orthodox Catholicism. My own definition of orthodox Catholicism encompasses obedience to all Church teachings and to the Holy Father as the successor of Peter even when he teaches at the ordinary level on matters of doctrine or morals. The Pope does not have to invoke infallibility every time he teaches in order to obtain our attention and to be taken seriously by us. I had conveniently ignored this fact during my liberal years. I know the early Jewish Christians never heard of infallibility. Yet they knew when Peter and the Apostles spoke they did so with the authority given by Christ. These Jewish Christians joyfully accepted the Apostle's teachings and authority. As a conservative Catholic (after my baptism), I followed the Church's moral and doctrinal teachings but decided for myself which social teachings I would honor. When I became liberal I followed the Church's doctrinal and social teachings and decided upon which moral teachings I would comply. Now I follow all the Church's and Pope John Paul's teachings, doctrinal (such as ordination of women), moral (birth control, abortion, capital punishment, euthanasia), social (racism, war, poverty) and disciplinary (such as priestly celibacy). And this brings me the peace and comfort I never truly enjoyed before. Love, forgiveness, humility, and compassion must also be the attributes of Catholic orthodoxy no matter how difficult life becomes. I now believe and I will publicly witness that our Holy Father, John Paul II, is one of the greatest Popes in the history of the Church.

Many blame the Second Vatican Council for all that seems wrong with the Church today including fewer vocations, fewer devotions (such as praying the rosary, adoration), fewer people going to Confession, high divorce rates, crisis in obedience to Church authority, decline in devotion to our Blessed Mother, general decline in morality, and many other things. Under the inspiration of the Holy Spirit, Pope John XXIII, Pope Paul VI, and the Council Fathers wanted to revitalize the Church by recalling its rich traditions thereby helping the faithful develop a closer relationship with our Lord and with each other as the people of God within the World. The document called "The Constitution on the Church" is the principal achievement of Vatican II. This self-reflection of the Church on her own nature formed the basis for the reform and renewal of Catholic life, which was the purpose of the entire Council. For me, this stands as one of the greatest councils in the history of the Church. The Church was in need of renewal. Renewal has been an ongoing event dating back to the First Council in Jerusalem some eighteen years after the death and resurrection of our Lord. Over the last twenty years, many conservative Catholics have felt this Council was unnecessary and only added confusion as to what the Church really believed and professed as her mission. Many liberal Catholics believe this Council provided them the opportunity to change or even ignore certain Church doctrines and laws, or pick and choose which ones to follow. The Second Vatican Council did not intend to dilute the teaching authority of the Church or change religious practices and rites (such as saying the Mass in English) just for the sake of change.

If many Catholics think the Second Vatican Council was responsible for many of the problems in the Church today, reflect with me for a few moments how the early Jewish Christians might have felt after the Council of Jerusalem in 51 A.D. This Council, in which all the Apostles participated under the leadership of St. Peter, decreed that circumcision, dietary regulations, and various other prescriptions of Mosaic Law were not obligatory for gentile converts to the Christian community. Participants issued the crucial decree in opposition to Judaizers who contended that observance of Mosaic Law in its entirety was necessary for salvation. What a blow this must have been for many Jews. They had lived their entire lives strictly according to Mosaic Law because they were taught and believed this was God's will as outlined in the books of the Old Testament, especially the Torah. Is it any wonder then, why many Jews rejected Jesus and His Church as a result of this Council? I cannot help but wonder if Catholics living today who feel betrayed by their Church as a result of Vatican II, and refuse to accept the changes, would have felt the same way had they been Jewish Christians in 51 A.D. And subsequently, would they have rejected Jesus and the authority of the Apostles? The problems we face today are not the result of this Council but a lack of real understanding what the Council formulated and promulgated by many clergy and laity, both conservative and liberal. To put an end to all the confusion help finally arrived. In 1992 our Holy Father released for publication the new *Catechism of the Catholic Church,* the first universal catechism in 400 years. In his "Apostolic Constitution *Fidei Depositum* On The Publication of the *Catechism of the Catholic Church,*" issued on October 11,1992, our Holy Father states:

> In 1985, I was able to assert, 'For me, then — who had the special grace of participating in it and actively collaborating in its development — Vatican II has always been, and especially during these years of my Pontificate, the constant reference point of my every pastoral action, in the conscious commitment to implement its directives concretely and faithfully at the level of each Church and the whole Church.

In this spirit, on January 25,1985, I convoked an extraordinary assembly of the Synod of Bishops for the 20th anniversary of the close of the Council. The purpose of this assembly was to celebrate the graces and spiritual fruits of Vatican II, to study its teaching in greater depth in order that all the Christian faithful might better adhere to it and to promote knowledge and application of it.

On that occasion the Synod Fathers stated: Very many have expressed the desire that a catechism or compendium of all catholic doctrine regarding both faith and morals be composed, that it might be, as it were, a point of reference for the catechisms or compendiums that are prepared in various regions. The presentation of doctrine must be biblical and liturgical. It must be sound doctrine suited to the present life of Christians. APler the Synod ended, I made this desire my own, considering it as fully responding to a real need of the universal Church and of the particular Churches.

For this reason we thank the Lord wholeheartedly on this day when we can offer the entire Church this reference text entitled the *Catechism of the Catholic Church* for a catechesis renewed at the living sources of the faith!

Following the renewal of the Liturgy and the new codification of the canon law of the Latin Church and that of the Oriental Catholic Churches, this catechism will make a very important contribution to that work of renewing the whole life of the Church, as desired and begun by the Second Vatican Council.'

After many years, it finally took our Blessed Mother's messages at Medjugorje to make me realize that no person probably understands the Church better in all its richness, and tries to guide us accordingly, than our Holy Father John Paul II. Since 1981 Mary has been teaching us how we as individuals need to change in order to bring a sinful world to the knowledge of her Son, Jesus. In all these years, She has never blamed Vatican II for all the ills in the Church or the world today. On the contrary, her messages sound in tune with the teachings of that Council.

As with the new *Catechism of the Catholic Church,* the messages of Mary cannot just be read. They must be seriously studied and supported by a lot of prayer. They must become an integral part of our lives. Our Lady gave the following message to one of the visionaries on December 25,1989:

...little Children, read everyday the messages I gave you and transform them into life. I love you and this is why I call you to the way of salvation with God.

Even if the Church's judgement on Medjugorje turns out to be negative, I would still continue to do all these things that bring me the peace of Jesus. After all, which of those things that I am now doing, as a result of Mary's messages, would the Church ask me to stop doing?

In July 1991, Sara left her job at the National Conference of Catholic Bishops. She wanted to get directly involved with helping people so she began working as a volunteer for our county government. She assists in the handling of abuse cases (children and women) involving Hispanics. The tragic situations Sara has dealt with are enough to challenge anyone's sanity. The sad part is the large number of abused persons who are not being helped due to lack of funding and, consequently, not enough paid staff professionals. If Sara did not go to daily Mass and pray the Rosary, she would probably be a "basket case" herself. Her devotion to our Lady is what keeps her going despite the misery she encounters. In a quiet way Sara lives our Lady's messages and shares them with the people she helps. She is also an inspiration to her fellow workers as well as to me.

Our Blessed Mother has given messages on many subjects. As a Jewish convert I see much of the beauty that the Catholic Church radiates and the words our Blessed Mother conveys as being rooted in Judaism. This is no surprise, considering Her own Jewish background. After Sara and I returned from our last trip to Medjugorje I started writing articles on various subjects about which our Blessed Mother spoke. I wrote from the perspective of my orthodox Jewish training, experience, subsequent conversion, and life as a Catholic. In 1991 I wrote a reflection called "The Holy Rosary, Rich in Jewish Tradition." Our Blessed Mother stressed the importance of praying the Rosary in the following messages:

Dear children, today I call you to begin to pray the Rosary with a living faith. That way I will be able to help you. You, dear children, wish to obtain graces, but you are not praying. I am not able to help you because you do not want to get started. Dear children, I am calling you to pray the Rosary and that your Rosary be an obligation which you shall fulfill with joy. That way you shall understand the reason I am with you this long. I desire to teach you to pray. (June 12,1986)

I wish only that for you the Rosary become your life.
(August 4, 1986)

Keep on praying that my plans be completely realized. I request the families of the parish to pray the Family Rosary.
(September 27, 1984)

Pray at least an entire Rosary: Joyous, Sorrowful and Glorious Mysteries. (August 14,1984)

One day while praying the Rosary, the real beauty of this prayer became especially evident to me. All the important elements of Jewish belief are rooted in the Rosary. The Rosary clearly shows me that Jesus is indeed the fulfillment of the promise made to Israel. The more time spent with our Lord in prayer, the greater the insights on His love and mercy. That's how the Holy Spirit works. Many books and articles have been written on the history of the Rosary, its meaning, and instructions for praying the mysteries. One of the best remains, "The Secret of the Rosary," by St. Louis De Montfort. I could not add anything to the great works on the Rosary. I wrote this reflection to share with others some insights on the Rosary that came to me from my background, first, as a Jew and, then, as a Catholic. Each day I pray the Rosary these insights (as well as those from other sources and the Scriptures) help me draw closer to Jesus and Mary, making me realize how blessed I am to have been born and raised as an Orthodox Jew and then given such a tremendous grace to know Jesus as my Savior and God, and Mary as my Mother.

With the help of the Holy Spirit, I pray that I can share with others the beauty that is the Catholic Church when it is seen together with our Lord as the fulfillment of the promise God made to Israel. I pray that this book might help others to see this. It is important for all of us to share our faith experiences in writing, speaking, or just by the example of how we live in the love of Jesus. You would be amazed at the results the Holy Spirit can achieve even with the poorest of instruments. That is why I put so much trust in Him to help me.

CHAPTER 7
THE BLESSED MOTHER'S CALL TO HOLINESS IN MEDJUGORJE

Our Mother calls all of us to prayer and conversion. Unfortunately, many people with good intentions, who have been to Medjugorje and organizations dedicated to spreading devotion to our Lady and to the Church fail to focus on the heart of our Blessed Mother's message. Instead, they pay attention to: (1) secrets (about future events) given to the visionaries soon after the apparitions began in 1981, (2) coming chastisement of God because of pervasive sin in the world, (3) sun spinning and rosaries turning color, and (4) miraculous cures.

Miraculous events validate the authenticity of apparitions. I have seen the miracle of the sun. My rosary changed color, and I know personally of two cures which I consider miraculous. But, some of the more vocal faithful seem to concentrate on these events, thereby offending many clergy, religious, and laity regarding Medjugorje. Yet Mary does not mention any of these occurrences in Her weekly and monthly messages conveyed through one of the visionaries named Marija. Our Lady gives these messages for the parish in Medjugorje and to all in the world who desire to live them. From March 1, 1984, to January 8, 1987, the messages were given weekly. Since January 25, 1987, they have been presented by our Mother (and still are) on the twenty-fifth of each month. I would now like to summarize some of the major themes in Mary's messages.

PRAYER: Pray, pray, pray. Pray with the heart, not only in words. Pray as a family. Need Prayer to comprehend God and Mary's plans and love for us. Ask for perseverance in prayer. Pray for outpouring of the Holy Spirit. Pray for enlightenment by the Holy Spirit. Pray before the Cross. No peace without prayer. Need prayer to overcome sin in the world. Pray to overcome trials. Pray for fulfillment of God's plan for parish (Medjugorje) and the world. Defeat every work of Satan through prayer. Pray for our neighbors. Pray daily for the souls in Purgatory. Pray without ceasing. Pray for conversion of all people to God. Prayer should be our joy. Prayer for us should take the first place. Always begin and end each day in prayer. By our prayer and our life we can help destroy all that is evil in others and uncover Satan's deception. We should consecrate ourselves to prayer with special love.

CONVERSION: Calls for conversion of parish and all other people. Calls us to listen and live the messages. Calls us to holiness, goodness, obedience and God's love. Calls us to grow in holiness. God will work through us and will keep giving us what we need (see Matthew 6:24-34.) God gives us free will which we control. Without us, God cannot bring to reality that which He desires. Lent provides special incentive for us to change. Don't be absorbed with material goods. We must surrender ourselves totally to God.

MARY: Consecrate ourselves to Mary. Jesus bestows special graces through Her. Mary loves us always, even when separated from Jesus and Her. She doesn't force anyone to accept Her messages. Give Mary all our feelings and problems. She comforts us in our trials; She loves all people the same. She forgives easily and is happy for all who return to Her. Abandon our hearts to Her so She can lead us further in love. Give Her our hearts so She can change them to be like Hers. Lord allows Her to intercede for more graces for us. Mary is the Mediatrix between us and God. Mary is with us, but She cannot take away our freedom to sin. She asks us to consecrate our lives to Her with love so She can guide us with love. She wants to lead us to holiness to Jesus. She protects us with Her motherly mantle. Our Mother and the Queen of Peace. Calls us to the Consecration of Her Immaculate Heart.

LOVE/JOY/HUMILITY: We must love. Begin in family, then everyone in parish, then all others. Through love we will achieve everything and even what we think impossible. Stop slandering. Love neighbor and those who do evil to us. The more we love our neighbor, the more we shall experience Jesus. Surrender ourselves completely to God. Live messages in humility. Without love we are unable to accept Jesus or Mary and cannot give an account of our experiences to others. Let the family be a harmonious flower. Live in mutual love. Overcome every sin with love. Live love within ourselves. Let our only instrument always be love. God wishes us to do works of love and mercy. Love bears everything bitter and difficult for sake of Jesus Who is love.

MASS: The greatest of all prayers. Mary calls us to a more active attendance at Holy Mass. Mass should be an experience of God. Show our love for Mary by going to Mass. Consciously live the Holy

Mass and let our presence be joyful. Come to Mass with love and make it our own. Holy Mass should be our life.

ROSARY: Pray at least one rosary (mystery) each day. Pray Rosary as family. Rosary can defeat Satan. Pray Rosary with a living faith. Let Rosary be an obligation which we shall fulfill with joy. Rosary is sign to Satan that we belong to Mary.

EVANGELIZATION: Live messages and convey them to all. Let all people be an example to others by their lives and let them witness to Jesus. Give the gifts we receive from God to others with love, not keeping them for ourselves. Be the light for everyone and give witness in the light. In everything, be an image for others, especially in prayer and witnessing. By our own peace, help others to see and begin to seek peace.

SATAN: Satan is real and very strong. Mary prays for us when tempted by Satan. Satan wants to destroy God's plan for the world. Do not allow Satan to get control of our hearts. By love, turn everything into good which Satan desires to destroy and possess. Our sacrifices for God can drive away Satan. Satan is a seducer.

SUFFERING/TRIALS: Persevere in suffering. Offer suffering as sacrifice to God with love. God tests us because He loves us. Be open to God and approach Him with love during trials. God will reward our sacrifices. He wants our sufferings to be a joy. He desires that our cross be a joy for us. Accept sickness and suffering with love the way Jesus accepted them. God is close to us and hears our prayers when we are sick, have problems, or encounter difficulties.

PENANCE: The Lord desires to purify us from all our past sins. Pray without ceasing and prepare our hearts in penance. Ask God's forgiveness for our sins. Avoid sin. Go to frequent Confession (Blessed Mother recommends monthly Confession).

CROSS/WOUNDS OF JESUS: Cross should be central in our lives. Make special consecration to Cross in our homes. Honor wounds of Jesus. Reflect on Jesus' passion and in our lives be united with Him.

FASTING: Fast strictly on Fridays. Bread and water (if health permits) is the best fast. Fasting helps in fulfillment of God's plan.

SCRIPTURE: Read the Bible every day. Bible should be displayed in a prominent place in our homes.

ADORATION: Adore the Blessed Sacrament. Venerate the Heart of Jesus. Mary invites us to glorify Jesus with Her.

THANKSGIVING: For all fruits, even little ones, thank God and glorify Him. Give thanks unceasingly for all we possess.

It is no coincidence that all the messages Mary brings us can be found in the Scriptures (especially Matthew chapters 5-7), in Church teachings (especially Vatican Council II) and the new *Cafechism of fhe Cafholic Church*. They call all of us to holiness through conversion. However, conversion requires effort on our part and an openness to the Holy Spirit.

CHAPTER 8
PRAY, PRAY, PRAY

It is very clear that the messages of our Blessed Mother to the visionaries in Medjugorje call for a greater quantity, intensity, and quality of prayer than ever before. Mary has spoken of the necessity of prayer to sustain a living faith, saying, **"faith cannot be alive without prayer."** Prayer is an essential means in attaining the peace of Christ in our hearts.

Several of the messages have simply been a repeated exhortation for more prayer, as seen in the message on April 19,1984:

> **Dear children, sympathize with Me. Pray, pray, pray!**

A later message asked for a decrease in work and an increase in prayer:

> **These days you have been praying too little and working too much. Pray, therefore. In prayer you will find rest.** (July 5,1984)

Active prayer is a necessity in living the full message of Medjugorje:

> **Dear children, I am calling you to an active approach to prayer. You wish to live everything I am telling you, but you do not get results from your efforts because you do not pray. Dear children, I beg you: open yourselves and begin to pray. Prayer will be joy. If you begin, it will not be boring because you will pray with pure joy.** (March 20,1986)

Mary specifically set the amount and degree of prayer for a youth prayer group in Medjugorje that began in June 1983:

> **Pray three hours a day...You pray too little. Pray at least half an hour in the morning and evening; and further when I say, 'pray, pray, pray,' I do not mean only to increase the hours of prayer but increase the desire to pray and to be in contact with God, to be in a continuous prayerful state of mind.**

To Catholics, the call to three hours of daily intensive prayer must be a shocker. After all, the Church only requires that we attend Mass on Sundays and holy days of obligation. And many are annoyed if the Mass lasts more than an hour. For many Catholics today, prayers like the Rosary, Benediction, and Adoration of the Blessed Sacrament belong to an earlier unenlightened age. People are much busier now with work, meetings, sports, socials, education needs, Little League, and exercise. For some of us there are even ministries. Many help in nursing homes, soup kitchens, liturgy committees, religious education, and other lay ministries in their Parish Church. Who has time for three hours of prayer? Is the Blessed Mother unreasonable in Her request? Several years ago my first inclination would have been that Mary could not expect that of each of us. And then as I studied and reflected on what Mary was asking of us through these young people and started to pray more each day, I knew once again not only was it possible, but it was a must if I was to understand God's will for me. Today, the world is impressed with the unselfish work of Mother Teresa and her Sisters among the poorest of the poor. Yet they could not be Jesus to the poor and rejected and do the works of mercy without daily Mass, prayer, the Rosary, frequent Confession, fasting, Adoration of the Blessed Sacrament, and reading Scripture. Mother Teresa and her Sisters live the message of Mary in Medjugorje.

I should have known that Mary's request was not unreasonable, recalling the years I had lived as a Jew. The belief and customs of Orthodox Jews today remain similar to the Pharisaic Jew in Jesus' time. It should be noted that our Lord did not condemn what Pharisees believed. He condemned the hypocrisy many of them practiced. A Jew has no problem understanding the need for three hours of daily prayer. I would like to describe what for many Orthodox Jews is a typical weekday prayer routine. There is the daily morning prayer service at the synagogue, which lasts about a half hour. Then a noonday service. And then there is the evening worship service in the synagogue. Ten men (above the age of 13) must be present in order to say all the prayers. For example, the **"Holy, Holy, Holy is the Lord of Hosts: the whole earth is full of His glory"** cannot be said if ten men are not present. If a Jew could not get to the synagogue he would pray the daily services (i.e., the parts one is allowed to pray) at home. The Sabbath, which is a very holy day, starts Friday evening with one-and-a-half hour service. Saturday morning the worship lasts about three hours. In the afternoon one comes back to the synagogue and discusses the Torah and the Talmud for several hours with the rabbi. The Sabbath ends with the evening service which lasts about two hours. On Yom Kippur, the Day of Atonement, a Jew fasts for more than 24 hours, with no food or drink of any kind. He spends all day praying in the synagogue from morning until after sundown. And no one complains.

Jews have been persecuted for centuries. For Jews there has not been a prophet in over 2,000 years to encourage them in their fidelity to God. There have been no miraculous events for Jews such as Lourdes, Fatima, and Medjugorje since Old Testament days. During World War II six million Jews living in Christian countries were annihilated. Yet, Orthodox Jews, who make up only about 10 percent of all Judaism, persist in their faith in God and still believe that He will send them their messiah. This is what the power of many hours of daily prayer can accomplish for those still faithful to the old covenant. Can you even imagine what it can do for us who have been blessed to be part of the new covenant that Christ established?

The peace I now have as a result of prayer cannot be adequately described. Yet I must never become content with the peace I enjoy. My prayer life must not only continue to increase but the quality must also keep improving. With the help of the Holy Spirit and His spouse, our Lady, I will be able to do this. I still have a lot of work to do in this area. But it is worth it, because I have experienced what it means to live without prayer being an integral part of my daily life. I also know that I can only share the peace I have now with others if they are willing to give our Lord the prayer time and quality He asks for. Seeing the miracle of the sun, rosaries turning color, or being overly obsessed regarding the secrets Mary has revealed to the visionaries will not give us peace and the understanding of God's will for each of us. We have to give ourselves completely in prayer to our Father.

The Mass is the greatest of all prayers. Since the Second Vatican Council many Catholics complain about the Mass. They do not like the fact that the Mass is no longer said in Latin, resulting in the loss of a sense of mystery. For others the Mass is dull and they do not get anything out of it. I think one of our problems today is that we like to be entertained. We do not want to be bored. For some, going to Mass should be a "fun" experience. When the celebration of Mass does not meet our expectations we seem to blame everything else but ourselves. When asked about the Mass during the first years of the apparitions in Medjugorje, Our Blessed Mother responded,

The Mass is the greatest prayer from God, and you will never understand the greatness of it.

That we understand the words of the Mass and their significance is most important regardless the language we pray the Mass. Although the Latin Mass should be preserved, our Blessed Mother has never said in any of Her messages, that the Church was wrong in replacing Latin in the Mass with the vernacular. If we really believe and understand that the Eucharist is our Lord's great undeserved free gift of Himself to us, the words by the priest, **"This is My Body — This is the cup of My Blood,"** alone would be enough to invoke in each of us feelings of great joy, peace, love, and, yes, even mystery. We would then not have to plan liturgies with all kinds of gimmicks to satisfy us in order to keep our interest or attention for the little enough time the Church asks us to come and worship our God. Then people would never say, "I do not have to go to Mass; I can pray at home or anywhere." On April 3, 1986, our Blessed Mother said in Her weekly message,

> **Dear children, I wish to call you to a living of the Holy Mass. There are many of you who have sensed the beauty of the Holy Mass, but there are also those who come unwillingly. I have chosen you, dear children, but Jesus gives you His graces in the Mass. Therefore, consciously live the Holy Mass and let your coming to it be a joyful one. Come to it with love and make the Mass your own.**

As a Jew, the joyous celebration of the Passover allowed me, once a year, to thank God for freeing my ancestors and myself from slavery in Egypt, for bringing us to the promised land, and for the hope of the coming of the Messiah. As a Catholic, the daily celebration of the Mass makes it possible for me to thank Jesus each day for allowing me to share in His Life now.

The Mass is also a community prayer. I said earlier, ten men were required to say certain prayers in the Jewish worship service. Maybe this was God's way of telling us if we were truly His people we had to worship Him together as a people. God calls us to community worship as well as to personal and private devotion. Private devotions such as the Rosary, spending time with Jesus in the Blessed Sacrament, reading Scripture, and listening to sacred music while driving in a car are some of the things we can do daily as forms of prayer. We are called to pray with great joy. Then, only then, will we be able to experience the peace that only Christ can give.

Although once again, I am experiencing the peace of Jesus in my life, it does not mean the end of suffering. If anything, as I grow closer to our Lord through prayer, I expect suffering to increase and be a part of my life until the day I go to meet Jesus and Mary. Prayer helps me understand Jesus' great love and mercy through which He allows us, by acceptance of our suffering, to share in His passion and death. For me, the shortest path to heaven is the road to Calvary, which follows the way of the cross.

The following scripture reading sums up for me the attitude Jesus expects me to have when I approach Him in prayer.

> He spoke the following parable to some people who prided themselves on being virtuous and despised everyone else. Two men went up to the temple to pray, one a pharisee, the other a tax collector. The pharisee stood there and said this prayer to himself, 'I thank you, God, that I am not grasping, unjust, adulterous like the rest of mankind, and particularly that I am not like this tax collector here. I fast twice a week; I pay tithes on all I get.' The tax collector stood some distance away, not daring even to raise his eyes to heaven; but he beat his breast and said, 'God, be merciful to me, a sinner.' This man, I tell you, went home again at rights with God; the other did not. For everyone who exalts himself will be humbled, but the man who humbles himself will be exalted. (Luke 18: 9-14)

Our Blessed Mother encourages us to pray as a family daily and to form or join prayer groups. Sara and I are part of a prayer group. On my second trip to Medjugorje in 1989 I met Bill and Terry Voss and Terry's mother, Kitty Sommer, also from the Suburban Maryland area. After Sara and I returned from our last pilgrimage in 1990, the five of us decided to form a prayer group. We were joined by Kitty's husband Helmut and Irene Williams. Helmut and Irene had not been to Medjugorje but were familiar with happenings there. Later Paul and Vivian Landis and Elly Andree joined us. We meet once a week, usually in the Sommers' house for an hour and a half. We pray a scriptural Rosary, after which I briefly comment on the following Sunday's Scripture readings. We then offer up petitions and close by chanting the Divine Mercy Chaplet (to be discussed in chapter 10). A prayer group should also be a support group. If enough prayer groups can be formed, I know there can be a dramatic return to God and an end to the great immorality now sweeping out of control all over the world.

CHAPTER 9
LOVE, FORGIVENESS, AND PRO-LIFE

In July 1990, Sara and I visited Poland as part of a pilgrimage tour with Archbishop Maida of Detroit. It was my first visit back since I was a 4-year-old child visiting my grandparents in Krakow. While in Poland we went to Auschwitz, the notorious concentration camp. It was an extremely emotional experience for me. Two of my aunts and their families were killed there. I saw pictures of little children (about 3 to 8 years old) who died in Auschwitz. Items on display included shoes, clothing, and other articles of the children. I realized then that but by the grace of God, and for what purpose He alone knows, I could have been in those pictures and my shoes and belongings could have been in that pile. Once again, I was reminded: how precious is the gift of life and to what lengths we must go to protect it.

Two thoughts stirred constantly in my mind from my trip to Auschwitz. One, love and forgiveness of one's enemies and, second, the meaning of life. I decided to write two articles dealing with these subjects. They are so important for us today that I would like to share my thoughts on them. Our Blessed Mother's messages often deal with these same subjects.

LOVE & FORGIVENESS

For many years of my life as a Jew I tried to hold to the Mosaic Code. During and after college I became lax in my religious practices because I felt my life style made it difficult for me to fit into the modern world. At the time of my entrance into the Catholic Church in 1963, I felt a great sense of relief. As a Catholic I did not have to follow the Mosaic Code nor have any more guilt feelings for not doing so. I felt Catholic laws and teachings were much easier for me to follow than the 613 commandments derived from Mosaic law.

My relief, however, was short-lived. I came to realize what Jesus expects of Christians is far more difficult than living according to Mosaic law. We read in Matthew 5 the following:

> For I tell you, if your virtue goes no deeper than that of the scribes and Pharisees, you will never get into the kingdom of heaven. (v.20)

> You have learnt how it was said: Eye for eye and tooth for tooth. But I say this to you: offer the wicked man no resistance. On the contrary, if anyone hits you on the right cheek, offer him the other as well. (v. 38-39)

> You have learnt how it was said: You must love your neighbor and hate your enemy. But I say this to you: love your enemies and pray for those who persecute you; in this way you will be sons of your Father in heaven, for he causes his sun to rise on bad men as well as good, and his rain to fall on honest and dishonest men alike. For if you love those who love you, what right have you to claim any credit? Even the tax collectors do as much, do they not? And if you save your greetings for your brothers, are you doing anything exceptional? Even the pagans do as much, do they not? You must therefore be perfect just as your heavenly Father is perfect. (v.43-48)

I had not paid as much attention to these teachings of Jesus as I should have during my conversion experience because, sad to say, I did not see them reflected in the lives of many Christians. To me Christians seemed no more loving or forgiving than any other people. I felt many Christians had a special hatred for Jews, in particular. For centuries now Jews have been persecuted by Christians. Jews have been accused of killing Christ and of all kinds of unscrupulous things. Even if it were true (which is not the case), where was Jesus' example of forgiveness and love that Christians should exemplify?

The commandments of Jesus — to love and forgive — did not hit home for me until I saw the relentless pursuit by some Jews to find and bring Nazis to justice. Within me a crisis formed. How could I forgive the Nazis who murdered in cold blood millions of people (including babies and children) during World War II? If by the grace of God my mother and I had not escaped from Germany in 1939, we would have been killed in one of the concentration camps along with many of my Jewish relatives. Despite all this, Jesus commands me to love my enemy and to forgive him. As a Christian I came to realize I had no choice but to forgive them and earnestly pray for their conversion. That is, I had no choice if I was a true follower of Jesus and wanted to share His Gospel with all people, especially sinners, which all of us are.

St. Aelred in his "Mirror of Love" sums up beautifully for me why the command of Jesus to love one another as He loved us is not just some theological ideal:

> The perfection of brotherly love lies in the love of one's enemies. We can find no greater inspiration for this than grateful remembrance of the wonderful patience of Christ. He who is more fair than all the sons of men offered his fair face to be spat upon by sinful men; he allowed those eyes that rule the universe to be blindfolded by wicked men; he bared his back to the scourges; he submitted that head which strikes terror in principalities and powers to the sharpness of the thorns; he gave himself up to be mocked and reviled, and at the end endured the cross, the nails, the lance, the gall, the vinegar, remaining always gentle, meek and full of peace. In short, he was led like a sheep to the slaughter, and like a lamb before the shearers he kept silent, and did not open his mouth. Who could listen to that wonderful prayer, so full of warmth, of love, of unshakable serenity - Father, forgive them and hesitate to embrace his enemies with overflowing love? Father, he says, forgive them. Is any gentleness, any love, lacking in this prayer?

To love and forgive does not mean that people should not be brought to justice if they are proven guilty of crimes. But we must love them and pray that the Lord will reconcile them to Himself. The thought of any soul spending eternity in Hell separated from God should be enough motivation for each of us to be models of Jesus' love and forgiveness so that His desire to save all His people can be accomplished through us. There is no other way He can do this. We are the only instruments He can use. Is that not the purpose of His Church? St. Paul writes in 2 Corinthians, chapter 5:

> From now onwards, therefore, we do not judge anyone by the standards of the flesh. Even if we did once know Christ in the flesh, that is not how we know him now. And for anyone who is in Christ, there is a new creation; the old creation has gone, and now the new one is here. It is all God's work. It was God who reconciled us to himself through Christ and gave us the work of handing on this reconciliation. In other words, God in Christ was reconciling the world to himself, not holding men's faults against them, and he has entrusted to us the news that they are reconciled. So we are ambassadors for Christ; it is as though God were appealing through us, and the appeal that we make in Christ's name is: be reconciled to God. For our sake God made

the sinless one into sin, so that in him we might become the goodness of God. (v.16-21)

Several years ago, the meeting between Pope John Paul II and Austrian President Kurt Waldheim upset many Jewish people. They felt that the Pope should not have met with a man who, while serving as an officer in the German Army, allegedly sent Jews to their death. Even if the allegations against Waldheim were true, the Holy Father would have had no choice but to meet with him. The Pope is, first of all, a Christian. But he is also a priest. And as such he has the power to forgive sin and must be available to any person who comes to him, no matter what that person was or is. Our Holy Father, the Vicar of Christ on earth, must be the model of Christ's love and forgiveness in the world.

Today, three quarters of the world's population is not Christian. And what do they see when they look at the Christian world? Do they see love and forgiveness? I am sure they hear (with help of the media who focus only on the bad news) about the hatred that exists between Orthodox Christians and Catholics in countries such as the Ukraine and former Yugoslavia. Many Protestants as well have not been good examples of Christian love and forgiveness. Even within the Catholic Church there are bitter divisions between liberals and conservatives. Too many Christians of all Churches exhibit openly, as well as subtly, prejudice of all sorts, racism, lack of charity, and hatred. Yet Christians enjoy pointing out the hypocrisy of the Pharisees when they confronted our Lord. But what about the modern day Christian pharisees who dare to pray **"...Forgive us our trespasses, as we forgive those who trespass against us..."** and fail to take these words of our Lord seriously in their everyday living.

Is there any hope for us then? Certainly. But I believe the only solution is to listen to and rally around another model, a most perfect model for all Christians and indeed all people, given to us by our Lord: His Blessed Mother Mary. Who in this world besides Jesus has ever suffered more than She did? She saw Her only Son brutalized and killed. Yet She loved and forgave all those who did that to Her Son. Who can show us the way to Jesus better than His Mother and our Mother? It is extremely urgent for us at this moment in history to change, to convert. That is why, unprecedented in Church history, She is appearing now in so many places throughout the world. In Medjugorje, She tells the visionaries the following regarding love and forgiveness:

My children, I thank you tor each sacrifice that you have made during these days. Be converted, forgive each other, fast, pray, pray, pray! (June 24,1984)

Dear children, I am calling you to the love of neighbor and love toward the one trom whom evil comes to you. In that way you will be able to discern the intentions of hearts. Pray and love, dear children! By love you are able to do even that which you think is impossible. (November 7,1985)

Dear children, I wish to thank you for all the sacrifices and I invite you to the greatest sacrifice, the sacrifice of love. Without love, you are not able to accept either me or my Son. Without love, you cannot give an account of your experiences to others. Therefore, dear children, I call you to begin to live love within yourselves. (March 27,1986)

No one said it would be easy to love and forgive especially those who are brutal, harm us, or hate us. Our Blessed Mother tells us it is a sacrifice. Considering the reward that can be gained for all God's people including ourselves, our Blessed Mother is asking very little of us. The reward for each of us is peace, the peace that only Jesus can give. However, we cannot achieve this peace if there is not total forgiveness in our hearts. Our salvation depends on our ability to forgive others. In Matthew chapter 6, Jesus tells us:

Yes, if you forgive others their failings, your heavenly Father will forgive you yours; but if you do not forgive others, your Father will not forgive your failings either. (v.14-15)

When each of us has the peace that Jesus gives, the Holy Spirit and our Blessed Mother will help us bring that peace to a world that desperately needs it. The future of all God's people depends on us, even if there are only relatively few at the moment who are willing to love as Jesus loved.

PRO-LIFE

Pope John Paul II has called abortion

one of the most dramatic problems of our age," in an address to several thousands of people on Italian Right to Life Day, Feb. 5, 1989. He said the "tuture of humanity is threatened... by wide-

spread recourse to abortion," and added: "A new culture of soli-
darity is needed. The life of everyone, even the life asking to be
born, even the life that is ill or weak or in decline, is an absolute
and inviolable good. (1990 Catholic Almanac)

During the last twenty years abortion has become one of the
most heatedly debated issues, many times stirring up highly emotional feelings and responses by those who are for or against it. In
some instances, abortion is the sole or main issue for candidates
running for elective office, whether at the city, state or federal level.
I believe it won't be long before euthanasia will also become a much
discussed issue. To a lesser extent capital punishment is also debated. Pro-life covers many areas, including abortion, capital punishment, euthanasia, world hunger/starvation, the poor, the homeless, and child abuse. As Christians we must be concerned about all
issues that affect life in its many phases.

I would like to share my views on abortion, capital punishment
and euthanasia. I am focusing primarily on these issues because I
believe that the taking of a life under any of these circumstances, at
least in a Judeo-Christian context, is clearly wrong and should be
condemned. I admit that during my life I have flip-flopped several
times on my position, not always agreeing with the Church's stand. It
took several years of intensive prayer as well as conversion, to make
me understand and accept the Church's position on these issues.

ABORTION

The following, taken from the 1990 *Catholic Almanac,* summarizes the Catholic Church's position on abortion.

Abortion is not only "the ejection of an immature fetus" from the
womb, but is "also the killing of the same fetus in whatever way
at whatever time from the moment of conception it may be pro-
cured." (This clarification of Canon 1398, reported in the Dec. 5,
1988 edition of L'Ossevatore Romano, was issued by the Pontifical Council for the Interpretation of Legislative Texts- in view of
scientific developments regarding ways and means of procuring
abortion.) Accidental expulsion, as in cases of miscarriage, is
without moral fault. Direct abortion, in which a fetus is inten-
tionally removed from the womb, constitutes a direct attack on
an innocent human being, a violation of the Fifth Commandment.
A person who procures a completed abortion is automatically
excommunicated (Canon 1298 of the Code of Canon Law); also

excommunicated are all persons involved in a deliberate and successful effort to bring about an abortion. Direct abortion is not justifiable for any reason, e.g.: therapeutic, for the physical and/or psychological welfare of the mother; preventive, to avoid the birth of a defective or unwanted child; social, in the interests of family and/ or community. Indirect abortion, which occurs when a fetus is expelled during medical or other treatment of the mother for a reason other than procuring expulsion, is permissible under the principle of double effect for proportionately serious reason; e.g., when a medical or surgical procedure is necessary to save the life of the mother.

Until 1945, the greatest holocaust of all time was the systematic and brutal murder of six million Jews by the Nazis. To that number must be added the murder of roughly six million other people. Today we are in the midst of a greater holocaust with seemingly no end in sight: the murder of millions of children each year in the womb of their mothers. Some Jews get very upset when Christians refer to abortion as a holocaust and compare it to the brutality of the Nazis against the Jewish people. For me, it is extremely sad that these Jews do not recognize the extent to which the world has succumbed regarding the killing of these helpless children, and that abortion is only an extension of what the Nazis started. I realize that for many their faulty thinking may stem from a lack of agreement as to the actual moment life begins. Does life begin at conception, three months after conception, or at birth? The Jew, the Christian and the Moslem — all believers in the one God Who alone is the author of all life — must always give the benefit of doubt to the child, that life begins at conception.

Today, in the Orthodox Jewish faith abortion is not an option except when a mother's life is threatened and after consultation with a physician. Long before I ever considered conversion to Christianity, I was against abortion for ANY reason. This stemmed from my understanding of the Orthodox Jewish faith and from the atrocities to the Jews in World War II. Since the time of Moses the Jewish faith has always treasured the value of life. Therefore, I cannot comprehend why there were so many Reform Jews in the forefront of the pro-abortion movement in the 1970's and still are. Some Reform Jews may disagree with me and say they are not pro-abortion but pro-choice. But how can any Jew, or at least one who claims to be a Jew (i.e., a follower of Moses and the prophets) ever be pro-choice, especially in light of the World War II holocaust? Jeremiah, one of the greatest Jewish prophets, writes the following in the Old Testament concerning his call by God.

> **The Word of Yahweh was addressed to me saying, 'Before I formed you in the womb I knew you; before you came to birth I consecrated you; I have appointed you as prophet to the nations'.**
> (Jeremiah 1 :4-5)

In as much as one of the creation accounts in the Old Testament book of Genesis imagined God as a potter (Genesis 2:7-8), the verb ('formed') took on the technical meaning "to create." After Jeremiah (approximately 550 BC), it became an accepted idea that God Himself formed the young child in the womb. The significance of this is that God knows us and stands as our unique master from the very first moment of our existence. Some other Old Testament writings that mention God forming life in the womb are: Psalms 22:9,10; 139:13-16; Isaiah 44:2,24; 49:5,15; Job 31:15. No one then has the right to terminate God's creation for any reason, except God.

If it is hard for me to accept a Jew as being pro-abortion or prochoice, it is still harder for me to understand how a Christian (Protestant, Catholic or Orthodox) can be pro- abortion or pro-choice. Since the 1960's over 30 million babies have been slaughtered in the womb of their mothers in the United States alone. How could I someday stand before Jesus, Who offered His own life for each of us in unconditional love, and tell Him to His face that I was pro-choice instead of pro-life? How can any Christian reflecting on Mary's visitation to Her cousin Elizabeth, as described in St. Luke's Gospel, not believe that a person already exists at the moment of conception? Almost immediately after Her conception Mary goes to visit and assist Her cousin Elizabeth who is six months pregnant. St. Luke in his Gospel gives us a vivid account of Mary's arrival at Elizabeth's house (Luke 1:39-58):

> **Now as soon as Elizabeth heard Mary's greeting, the child leapt in her womb and Elizabeth was filled with the Holy Spirit. She gave a loud cry and said, 'Of all women you are the most blessed, and blessed is the fruit of your womb. Why should I be honored with a visit from the mother of my Lord?'** (Luke 1:41-43)

Elizabeth didn't recognize that Mary's womb held a "fetus." No one less than God, the Holy Spirit, gave Elizabeth the gift to recognize that what was alive in her cousin's womb was already a person.

And that Person was her Lord (God). Luke also tells us that the child (not fetus) in Elizabeth's womb leapt for joy. Can any Christian still doubt that from the moment of conception a human person already exists?

Every woman's womb is potentially the place where God's holy creation of human life can mature until the time of birth. From the moment of conception a woman is in intimate contact with God's creative power within her. And when life begins to exist in the womb, it becomes a sacred place. No man can ever share that unique experience of God's presence. We hear from pro-choice and pro-abortion people that a woman has a right over her own body. How is this consistent with Judeo-Christian beliefs? St. Paul tells Christians in Philippians 2:4-8 to always consider others before themselves and that their attitude must be the same as Christ's.

How can this abortion holocaust be stopped? I personally believe things are so bad that only God's intervention can put an end to this great tragedy. However, for us Christians circumstances are never hopeless and we are never helpless. Although the Catholic Church's position on abortion is very clear, there are many priests, religious and laity who are either pro-choice or pro-abortion (under certain conditions). Possibly, they may even represent the majority within the Church. This is one of the reasons our Blessed Mother has been calling all of us to conversion in Medjugorje and many other places throughout the world for more than ten years.

Abortion raises two basic problems. The first is the murder of defenseless innocent children who should feel safe in their mothers' womb. The only consolation in this type of holocaust is that these aborted little ones probably go straight to God and eternal happiness. The second problem concerns the attitudes and beliefs of those having the abortion, those encouraging abortions, and those who perform or assist in abortions. How do we bring the love and forgiveness of Jesus to these people? How can we be instruments of their conversion? How can we become the evangelizers that Jesus expects us to be to these people? Can we do it through civil disobedience at abortion clinics? I don't think so, especially when I see the anger displayed by both pro-abortion and pro-life groups when they confront each other. Where there is anger or hatred, love cannot flourish. How much better it is to see groups lovingly and peacefully praying the rosary within the limits of the law for those who enter or work in abortion clinics, or even peaceful marches that demonstrate our love and concern for the unborn and also for those involved in their slaughter. I hope that we can come to understand that several hours a day spent in prayer is the kind of sacrifice that can convert the world. It allows God to act in His time and in His way. Relying heavily on prayer means putting all our trust in Him. And how tough it is to completely trust God! Many times people question why God takes so long to act when terrible things occur. Sometimes I hear the classical non-scriptural remark that God helps those who help themselves, and this philosophy becomes the justification for taking matters into one's own hands. Unfortunately, many times we rely on purely human methods and solutions which are not based on the Gospel or Church teachings.

CAPITAL PUNISHMENT

The following, taken from the 1990 *Catholic Almanac,* summarizes the Catholic Church's position on capital punishment.

The political community which has authority to provide for the common good, has the right to defend itself and its members against unjust aggression and may in extreme cases punish with the death penalty persons found guilty before the law of serious crimes against individuals and a just social order. Its value as a crime deterrent is a matter of perennial debate. The prudential judgment as to whether or not there should be capital punishment belongs to the civic community. Capital punishment was the subject of a statement issued March 1, 1978, by the Committee on Social Development and World Peace, U.S. Catholic Conference. The statement said, in part: "The use of the death penalty involves deep moral and religious questions as well as political and legal issues. In 1974, out of a commitment to the value and dignity of human life, the Catholic bishops of the United States declared their opposition to capital punishment. We continue to support this position, in the belief that a return to the use of the death penalty can only lead to the further erosion of respect for life in our society.

Years ago I was a firm believer in capital punishment. However, it was the abortion holocaust that made me rethink my views on this subject. The last few years of intensive prayer and reflection on our Blessed Mother's messages for conversion and peace have led me to conclude that capital punishment should never be implemented. In reaching this conclusion, I have also been guided by our Holy Father John Paul II's example of public pleas for clemency for many terrible criminals facing execution. One may question how taking the life of a murderer can be compared to the killing of an innocent child in the womb. Please note, I believe strongly that a murderer must be punished for taking a life. Justice and good order require it, but Christian justice should never resort to any form of violence to accomplish its goal. Capital punishment is violent because it means the killing of life. A just punishment can be life imprisonment without parole. Our Lord desires the salvation of all people. He wants to give each person time to repent before he or she is called by Him. He has always gone out of His way to call the sinner back to Him. The greater the sinner, the greater the grace received from God in order to repent. A murderer who is imprisoned for life would have plenty of opportunity to repent, convert to God and receive eternal life. It would be the murderer's choice to respond. But the Church which includes clergy, religious and laity, needs to do a better job of evangelization and not be timid in proclaiming the Gospel of Jesus Christ. There was a time when I personally would have had no problem in killing Hitler or the Nazis who committed gross atrocities. Jesus, however, demands that we forgive and through love help even the most evil of persons repent and turn back to God. Our own salvation depends on our forgiving others.

Cardinal James Hickey, the Archbishop of Washington, issued the following statement in October 1992 opposing the District of Colombia's Death Penalty Initiative.

> The Catholic Church is opposed to the pending referendum calling for the reinstatement of the death penalty in the District of Columbia. Through its bishops, the Church has consistently called for a more humane, hopeful, and effective response to the violence in our streets than capital punishment. While we recognize that the state has the right to take the life of a guilty person of an extremely serious offense, the Catholic Bishops of the United States have declared their opposition to the death penalty in our country. Our 1980 Statement on Capital Punishment said: "We believe that, in the conditions of contemporary American society, the legitimate purposes of punishment do not justify the imposition of the death penalty. Furthermore, we believe that there are serious considerations which should prompt Christians and all Americans to support the abolition of capital punishment." Here in the District of Columbia, those "serious considerations"

must include the disproportionate infliction of the death penalty on minority and disadvantaged persons, the unproven effectiveness of the death penalty in deterring criminal behavior, and the absence in the proposed legislation of exemption for juveniles and mentally retarded persons. There is no doubt that the movement to reinstate the death penalty is a reaction to the increase in senseless and impersonal violence in the District of Columbia. We recognize this appalling trend. But the death penalty is not the answer. Answers lie in the reform of our legal and correctional systems, in the strengthening of family life, and in fostering a deep respect for the dignity of human life. And, above all, in prayer!

I hope that someday all the nations will heed the words of Cardinal Hickey. It is for the sake of the millions of children murdered in their mothers' wombs that I feel we must stand up now for the protection of all life, even the life of brutal butchers. Let us always keep in mind our Lord's words from His Sermon on the Mount:

Blessed are the merciful, for they shall obtain mercy.
(Matthew 5:7)

EUTHANASIA

The following passage taken from the 1990 *Catholic Almanac* summarizes the Catholic Church's position on euthanasia.

Mercy killing, the direct causing of death for the purpose of ending human suffering. Euthanasia is murder and is totally illicit, for the natural law forbids the direct taking of one's own life or that of an innocent person. The use of drugs to relieve suffering in serious cases, even when this results in a shortening of life as an indirect and secondary effect, is permissible under conditions of the double effect principle. It is also permissible for a seriously ill person to refuse to follow — or for other responsible persons to refuse to permit — extraordinary medical procedures even though the refusal might entail shortening of life.

A growing movement seems to be underway in this country to legalize euthanasia. There is even a Dr. Death who helps people (not necessarily those terminally ill) commit suicide. If euthanasia is legalized, it won't be long before such actions as those of Dr. Death will also become legal. Those who condone euthanasia want to be seen as compassionate, loving and merciful people. While those of us who believe only God can terminate life are portrayed as insensitive people without compassion for those who are suffering terribly from physical or mental problems. I never cease to be amazed how Satan can make good look bad and evil look good.

Many Christians have difficulty understanding that tremendous value can be derived by their sufferings not only for themselves but as a witness to others. If they would try to unite their pain and anguish to the passion of our Lord Jesus, they would experience the true peace that only God can provide. Such devotion takes education and lots of prayer. One does not learn about the redemptive value of suffering over night. Like conversion, it is usually a growing process. In praying the sorrowful mysteries of the Rosary I am continually reminded of Jesus' sacrifice for all of us. It gives me great comfort to know that if ever the time comes when I may have to endure great suffering, I will be united even more closely to Him. There was a time when Jews believed that when they suffered, the suffering was a sign of God's punishment due to their sins (see the Old Testament book of Job). Some Christian groups still believe this. Yet the suffering and death of our Lord Jesus disproves that belief. Our God is a God of love and mercy, but He expects Christians to follow His example and Gospel.

If euthanasia is legalized what will come next? The original purpose of the death camps built by the Nazis was to eliminate the mentally retarded, people with deformities and even German soldiers returning home from war who had been mutilated. After all the Aryan race must be pure. We know only too well that these death camps were eventually used for ethnic cleansing. Will we ever learn from history that when human life is threatened anywhere, it is threatened everywhere? Are we not witnessing once again ethnic cleansing in the former Yugoslavia?

I am concerned that the time is rapidly approaching when the majority of people will see euthanasia as a humane way to end suffering and thereby terminate life. They will be easily convinced that euthanasia is the compassionate and merciful thing to do especially when the quality of a particular life has reached a point where they feel it no longer has any meaningful value. Let any Christian who believes this go to Jesus hanging on the Cross and tell Him that. Can we ever learn that all life regardless of its condition is precious, holy and has great value?

My first wife Irma spent the last four months of her life in a hospital. Due to the effects of diabetes, her condition one month before her death, was as follows: although she was only 44 years old, her blood circulation system was like that of a 75 year old woman; she was unable to see anything, except for some light; as a result of one dialysis treatment, one of her legs had to be amputated; her kidneys were infected and failing; she was unaware of what was happening around her or recognized anybody even by voice. The doctors at the time did not know how long she could live. She could live one day, a month or a year. Only God knew. I was then asked to make one of the most difficult decisions of my life. The doctors asked me if they should use extraordinary means to keep her alive. After praying and getting Church guidance (although I was sure of the Church's position on this) I decided against the use of extraordinary means (other than water or food) to extend her life. This was also Irma's wish expressed several months earlier. Despite her worsening condition and the possibility that she could have remained that way for an extended period, I never considered asking the doctors to terminate her life. Irma also would never have wanted that. Only God had the right to decide the time and manner in which He would take her to Himself. If we ourselves decide the time for the direct termination of our lives or those of others, we may well end up in a place other than the one where God resides.

It is impossible to cover adequately such a complex topic as pro-life in a short reflection. I am confident, however, that the Holy Spirit and the Church can guide us if we are open to direction. Each one of us must form his or her own conscience on these issues. As Catholic Christians we cannot properly form that conscience and be true followers of Jesus, no matter how brilliant or educated we may be, without the guidance of the Church and lots of prayer. It is extremely important to remember and to stress that we as Christians are called not to judge or condemn those with whom we disagree, but rather, to be loving and forgiving persons, as taught by our Lord Jesus. Let our Blessed Mother Mary, the Mother of all people, always be our guide.

I do not want to leave the impression with you that I implied political action is not required regarding pro-life issues. I have only been trying to stress that without God's intervention no human action alone can bring about change, especially change of the heart. God wants our prayers and conversion in order for Him to intervene. However, as Americans we must exercise our rights to encourage legislation through the legal process that reflects our Christian moral values. I do not consider this forcing my beliefs on others provided I respect their voting rights as well as the beliefs and freedom of all people. No Catholic politician should be pro-choice. He or she must be pro-life even at the risk of losing an election. Jesus said,

> **What gain is there for a man to have won the whole world and to have lost or ruined his very self** (Luke 9:z5)

We must proclaim the Gospel by the example of our lives. Christians can evangelize the world by the way they live. And we must be loving, compassionate and forgiving no matter how difficult this may be.

CHAPTER 10
DIVINE MERCY

The ancient Hebrew religion was not merely a religion of fear before the divine majesty as many have claimed. It was a religion which also expressed God's merciful love. Throughout the Old Testament the mercy of God is stressed. The richness of this divine mercy is gradually unfolded, until it reaches its climax with the coming of Christ.

The manifestation of divine mercy reaches its height first in the birth of the God-Man, Jesus Christ, at Bethlehem and in His redemption of mankind through His passion and death; secondly, in the call of the Gentiles or pagans to the Christian faith; thirdly, in the future conversion of Israel to acknowledge Jesus as Messiah according to the prophecy of St. Paul; and finally in our being destined for eternal blessedness in heaven.

Since ancient times there is plenty of evidence in the Old Testament Scriptures for an all-good, merciful and forgiving God. Even after the sin of Adam and Eve, God sought to make them acknowledge their disobedience to His commandment, and then promised them a future Redeemer. Let us recall how God's mercy outstrips His justice. If He had found only 10 just men, He would have spared Sodom and Gomorrah from destruction despite their grievous sin (Genesis 18:16-33).

The entire history of Israel is a continuous chain of divine favors and blessings, and is a positive proof of God's mercy toward His chosen people of the Old Testament. The Hebrew nation, with whom God entered into a personal and special covenant on Mount Sinai, and to whom He gave the law through Moses, was the particular object of divine mercy because, as the prophet Jeremiah tells us,

He loved it with an everlasting love. (Jeremiah 31:3)

All the warnings of the divinely chosen prophets, as an Isaiah or a Jeremiah, an Amos or an Osee, all their terrible predictions of the divine impending judgment and punishment of the Hebrew nation were uttered to obtain a genuine and sincere repentance on the part of God's chosen people, so that He might show His mercy and pardon them. Isn't this the same call to us today of our Blessed Mother through the visionaries in Medjugorje?

During the time of the Babylonian exile (about 586-510 B.C.) God continually urged His chosen people to repent, so that He might shower His mercy upon them and so that His future blessings might become effective. It was only for a moment, says the prophet Isaiah, that He forsook them; but with great mercy He would bring them home again to Jerusalem (Isaiah 54:7). Even after the exile, when the people forgot their debt of gratitude to God as their Father and Master, He continued to shower His mercies upon them; as we are told by the Prophet Malachi (3:10,17).

Everywhere in the Old Testament we see the merciful Heart of God poured out upon individual souls; upon the poor, oppressed and suffering; upon truly repentant sinners who would rend their hearts in contrition, so that they could say with David that it is better to fall into the hands of God, whose mercies are many, than into the hands of men.

When we come to see the New Testament, we must observe that one of the most outstanding features in the life of Christ was His mercy and sympathy toward the miserable conditions of men, both physical and spiritual.

As Christ's mission was essentially spiritual, He showed, in particular, His deep sympathy toward repentant sinners. By forgiving their sins, He gave them renewed courage and strength to amend their lives and to make them pleasing to God. In the parable of the Prodigal son, the crown and pearl of all the parables of the Bible, we read of a son who turned his back on his own father and house, and yet when he repented, was welcomed with a greater expression of love and tenderness than if he had never done any wrong or gone away. This parable was intended to show the great truth of the inexhaustible love and mercy of the Heavenly Father for His sinful yet repentant child on earth; to exemplify the love and mercy which the Sacred Heart of Jesus had come to proclaim to mankind by His teachings and even more by His example.

On November 30,1980, Holy Father John Paul II issued his encyclical "Rich in Mercy". It is a document every Christian should read and reflect on. Pope John Paul II states:

Jesus Christ taught that man not only receives and experiences the mercy of God but that he is called to practice mercy toward others. Blessed are the merciful, for they shall obtain mercy. The

Church sees in these words a call to action, and she tries to practice mercy... Forgiveness demonstrates the presence in the world of the love which is more powerful than sin. Forgiveness is also the fundamental condition for reconciliation of God with man, but also in relations between people.

As mentioned above, the concept of "mercy" in the Old Testament has a long and rich history. The following are some excerpts from the encyclical taken from Chapter III entitled the Old Testament:

In the preaching of the prophets mercy signifies a special power of love, which prevails over the sin and infidelity of the chosen people.

Thus, in deeds and in words, the Lord revealed his mercy from the very beginnings of the people which he chose for himself; and, in the course of its history, this people continually entrusted itself, both when stricken with misfortune and when it became aware of its sin, to the God of mercies. All the subtleties of love become manifest in the Lord's mercy toward those who are his own: he is their Father for Israel is his first-born son. The Lord is also the bridegroom of her whose new name the prophet proclaims: Ruhamah, "Beloved" or "she has obtained pity."

Even when the Lord is exasperated by the infidelity of his people and thinks of finishing with it, it is still his tenderness and generous love for those who are his own which overcomes his anger. Thus it is easy to understand why the psalmists, when they desire to sing the highest praises of the Lord, break forth into hymns to the God of love, tenderness, mercy and fidelity.

The Old Testament encourages people suffering from misfortune, especially those weighed down by sin — as also the whole of Israel, which had entered into the covenant with God — to appeal for mercy, and enables them to count upon it: it reminds them of his mercy in times of failure and loss of trust. Subsequently, the Old Testament gives thanks and glory for mercy every time that mercy is made manifest in the life of the people or in the lives of individuals. In this way, mercy is in a certain sense contrasted with God's justice, and in many cases is shown to be not only more powerful than that justice but also more profound. Even the Old Testament teaches that, although justice is an authentic virtue in man, and in God signifies transcendent perfection, nevertheless love is "greater" than justice: greater in the sense that it is primary and fundamental. Love, so to speak, conditions justice and, in the final analysis, justice serves love.

Christ reveals the Father within the framework of the same perspective and on ground already prepared, as many pages of the Old Testament writings demonstrate. At the end of this revelation, on the night before he dies, he says to the Apostle Philip these memorable words: "Have *I* been with you so long, and yet you do not know me...? He who has seen me has seen the Father. (John 14:9)

In the course of history, whenever mankind was threatened with a crisis of a spiritual, social or political nature, God in His infinite mercy raised up visionaries to help people service it and even learn from it. In this century to counteract atheism, materialism and humanism, God sent the Blessed Virgin Mary to three children in Fatima and when Hitler was rising in power, Jesus Himself came to a Polish peasant girl known in religious life as Sister Faustina.

The following is taken verbatim from a booklet entitled "Devotion to the Divine Mercy" published by Marian Helper Center.*

"Sister Faustina was born Helena Kowalska in the village of Glogowiec near Lodz, Poland, the third of ten children. At the age of twenty, she entered the Congregation of the Sisters of Our Lady of Mercy, whose members devote themselves to the rehabilitation of wayward women and girls and to the care of girls exposed to situations dangerous to their morals. In 1934, obeying the wish of her spiritual director, Sister Faustina began keeping a personal diary which she entitled *Divine Mercy in my Soul*. It contains a detailed account of profound revelations and extraordinary spiritual experiences. It discloses how our Lord chose to entrust her with a very special mission, namely, to announce anew to mankind the Gospel message of His mercy, and to set forth new forms of devotion to God as Mercy for everyone, especially for those who need it most. In Sister Faustina's Diary we find many indications of that mission. On June 4,1937, she recorded: 'Today is the Feast of the Most Sacred Heart of Jesus. During Holy Mass I was given the knowledge of the Heart of Jesus and of the nature of the fire of love with which He burns for us and how He is an ocean of mercy. Then I heard a voice:

Apostle of My mercy, proclaim to the whole world My unfathomable mercy. Do not be discouraged by the difficulties you encounter in proclaiming My mercy. These difficulties that affect you so painfully are needed for your sanctification and as evidence that

---

* ©1993 Congregation of Marians, Stockbridge, Massachusetts 01262; printed with permission; all world rights reserved.

this work is Mine. My daughter, be diligent in writing down every sentence I tell you concerning My mercy, because this is meant for a great number of souls who will profit from it. (III,38)

Jesus is reported to have said to her on another occasion,

My daughter, secretary of My mercy, not only is it required of you to write about and proclaim My mercy, but draw down for them by your earnest supplications the grace that they too may glorify My mercy. (III,44)

At still another time He ordered her,

Write down everything that comes to mind regarding My goodness.

Sister Faustina reacted to these words of the Savior exclaiming, "How so, Lord; what if I write too much?" Jesus assured her,

My daughter, were you to speak with all the tongues of men and angels all at once you would still not say too much; indeed, you would only be extolling My goodness in an exceedingly small degree. She then begged, "O my Jesus, put words into my mouth Yourself so that I might praise You worthily." Jesus answered: My daughter, be at peace; do as I tell you. Your thoughts are united to My thoughts, so write whatever comes to your mind. You are the secretary of My mercy. I have chosen you for that office in this and the next life. That is how I want it to be in spite of all the opposition they will give you. Know that My choice will not change. (VI,9)

Sister Faustina died of multiple tuberculosis on October 5 ,1938, at the age of 33, on the eve of World War II, whose coming she had foretold and whose universal scope and horrors she had intimated to her sisters in religion. Through the message of mercy for which she lived, suffered and died she was Christ's provident instrument of comfort, encouragement and hope to mankind overwhelmed by that great calamity which it brought upon itself.

The great efficacy of the simple devotion to The Divine Mercy made known by her was the reason for its rapid spread throughout her native Poland, for its penetration into the horrendous prison camps scattered around the country and beyond it in all directions, and finally for its dissemination by refugees to all parts of the world.

Though prohibited by Church authorities for a while, again, as Sister Faustina had foretold to her spiritual director, the forms of the devotion revealed to her were once more permitted to be spread on April 15,1978. Six months later the champion of her cause was elevated to the Chair of Peter as Pope John Paul II; and after his recovery from an attempted assassination, at the Shrine of Merciful Love on the Feast of Christ the King, 1981, he was able publicly to declare:

> A year ago I published the encyclical 'Dives in Misericordia'. This circumstance made me come to the Sanctuary of Merciful Love today. By my presence I wish to reconfirm, in a way, the message of that encyclical. I wish to read it again and deliver it again. Right from the beginning of my ministry in St. Peter's See in Rome, I considered this message my special task. Providence has assigned it to me in the present situation of man, the Church and the world. It could also be said that precisely this situation assigned that message to me as my task before God...

The most important and most fundamental ingredient of the Divine Mercy devotion that must be basis for all the devotion's elements, is complete confidence, or trust, in Jesus. The Lord insists on this in very clear terms, as Sister Faustina noted in her Diary:

> No soul will be justified unless it turns with confidence to My Mercy (II, 39,40). [Let] the greatest sinners place their trust in My mercy. They have the right before others to confidence in the abyss of My mercy (III,39). Graces are drawn from [the fount of] My mercy with one vessel only, and that is - trust. The more a soul trusts, the more it will receive (V,148). I make myself dependent upon your trust; if your trust will be great, then My generosity will know no limits (II,19). Sins of distrust wound Me most painfully. (III,21)

All the forms of devotion to the Divine Mercy revealed to Sister Faustina, then, whether it be the veneration of the image of the Divine Mercy, or the recitation of the Chaplet, or receiving the Sacraments on the Feast of Mercy, are of value only to the degree that they are expressions of trust in Jesus - the Divine Mercy incarnate."

In our trip to Poland in 1990, Sara and I were privileged to be able to pray at the tomb of Sister Faustina in the Chapel of the Sisters of Mercy in Krakow. On April 18,1993, the first Sunday after Easter, a day our Lord told Sister Faustina He wanted officially established as a "Feast of Mercy" in the Church, she was beatified by Pope John Paul II.

I would strongly encourage people to obtain the "Devotion to the Divine Mercy" booklet and learn all the forms of devotion to the Divine Mercy and put them to practice. May I also recommend a book on the life of Sister Faustina entitled "Mercy My Mission" by Sister Sophia Michalenko, C.M.G.T. published by the Marian Press, Stockbridge, Mass. 01263.

The importance and need of the Church to bear witness to God's mercy is stated by our Holy Father:

> ...there comes to mind once more those words which, by reason of the incarnation of the son of God, resounded in Mary's Magnificat and which sing of 'mercy from generation to generation.' The church of our time, constantly pondering the eloquence of these inspired words and applying them to the sufferings of the great human family, must become more particularly and profoundly conscious of the need to bear witness in her whole mission to God's mercy, following the footsteps of the tradition of the Old and the New Covenant, and above all of Jesus Christ himself and his apostles.

CHAPTER 11
END TIMES

After His resurrection, Jesus showed His disciples He was alive by many proofs, appearing to them for forty days and speaking of the Kingdom of God. (Acts 1:3.) After all the time Jesus spent with them, the disciples still had difficulty comprehending that Jesus was not the type of messiah they had hoped for, but the suffering servant described by the prophet Isaiah in chapter 53. They forgot the times Jesus told them that someday they too would have to carry crosses, suffer hardships, and be killed. Still, just before the Ascension they asked Jesus,

> **Lord, has the time come? Are you going to restore the kingdom to Israel?** (Acts 1:6)

Since the time of Jesus' Ascension, Christians have been hoping and praying for His return. St. Paul, early in his ministry, believed that Jesus' return would be imminent, maybe even within his lifetime. How many predictions and "prophecies" regarding the beginning of end times described in the Bible have been made right down to today? Dates have come and gone and Jesus has not yet returned.

Is it possible, however, that we are indeed very close to our Lord's second coming? I personally believe that the return of our Lord will take place shortly. But I do not know when or what immediate effects it will bring about. I would like to address a number of factors that lead me to believe that we are about to witness the return of Christ and what we should be doing to prepare for it.

THE RETURN OF JESUS

In a recent message given to Marija in Medjugorje, our Blessed Mother said essentially that if we wish to discern what is going to unfold, reflect on the events taking place in the world, read the Scriptures, and pray. Events similar to those addressed below have always taken place throughout the course of history. But never have they happened so rapidly in such enormous proportions and been so widespread as in this century. And these events do not appear to have reached their peak. Many people are always looking to that one particular dramatic day that will signal Jesus' return. I think that His return will be preceded by a very violent and dramatic period, not necessarily one singular event. I also believe that this final period started at the beginning of the twentieth century and will shortly come to an end through a series of even more dramatic events. The happenings will clearly show everyone that God exists, is merciful, and might very soon render His judgement on us.

SCIENCE. This century has witnessed advances in technology and medicine that far exceed the total advances made previously since the creation of the universe. We now have capabilities that can extend life as well as its quality and at the same time can also destroy it in ways never imagined only one hundred years ago. In many instances the advances in science are keeping well ahead of the ethical and moral questions that need to be addressed as to how we use that science in certain instances. In other words, how do we distinguish between being enlightened by God to be creative and doing those things that belong only to God's domain? In most cases people are answering these questions for themselves because believers have no patience to wait for the Church's guidance and nonbelievers are not interested in any guidance. With the tremendous advances in worldwide communications (telephone, television, radio, newspapers, fax) it is possible to inform or mislead masses of people on events taking place anywhere in the world almost immediately.

WARS. Before this century there was never a world war. The twentieth century has had two. During World War I, more than 20 million people were killed. In that war, Christian countries fought Christian countries, almost two thousand years after the Prince of Peace came to redeem the world. In World War II, it is estimated that in excess of 40 million persons died. In a Christian country a vicious regime rose to power, which in the most sadistic way in all of history, systematically slaughtered more than 10 million people in gas chambers and through other unthinkable means. The Jewish people experienced a holocaust never before seen. Today, the slaughter continues in former Soviet Union countries, now independent, and in the former Yugoslavia and in Rwanda. Throughout the world potential trouble spots surface, such as North Korea, China, Cuba, and the Middle East. There is the constant threat of terrorist acts supported by several nations against innocent people. The Scriptures talk about terrible wars preceding end times. Can we expect worse yet to come than has already occurred in this century and is in fact still going on?

IMMORALITY. Since the fall in the Garden of Eden, immorality has plagued the family of man. Throughout history there have been those who had no regard for the sanctity of human life. But never has this disregard occurred on such grand scale. Let's take a quick look at society's actions during the last 25 years which shows no signs of diminishing.

1. Abortion. Since 1970 more than 30 million unborn babies have been slaughtered in their mothers' womb in the United States alone. And the killings continue at the rate of 1.5 million a year.
2. Divorce. Statistics claim that 50 percent of all marriages end in divorce. Is it any wonder, since many couples marry with the attitude that if it does not work they will break up?
3. Lifestyles. Today young people live together without contracting marriage and want the state to grant them the same benefits as married couples. Many consider sex outside of marriage, including adultery, as normal and not wrong. Many claim that sexually transmitted diseases can be prevented by giving everyone, especially teenagers, condoms. Gays want us to accept and approve of their lifestyles which fly in the face of Judaic-Christian moral teaching as well as the Scriptures. They also want the state to recognize homosexual marriages as it does heterosexual unions. And they tell us that we cannot be loving, caring, and forgiving people if we reject their behavior.
4. Drug and Crimes. The use of drugs and alcohol by young people as well as adults soars. In major cities the crime rate continues to mount and the number of murders committed set new records each year. Most prime TV shows seem to be dominated by sex and violence. After all, this sells.

In solutions proposed by politicians and socially minded people God is seldom mentioned. Is it possible that most people believe that all problems can be resolved without the help of God? Or maybe they believe that, except for crime, the above are not problems at all, but are part of an age that has finally attained enlightenment.

ATTACKS ON THE CHURCH AND THE VATICAN. Many nations and their leaders, as well as many Catholics, criticize and even condemn Pope John Paul II for his traditional stand on abortion, opposition to homosexual activity, divorce, contraception, celibacy, ordination of women, and other issues.

A Washington, DC-based group called Catholics for a Free Choice — that the nation's Bishops say is not an authentic Catholic organization — played a vocal role in the April 1994 preparatory meetings at the United Nations for the International Conference on Population and Development scheduled to be held in Cairo, Egypt, in September 1994. "Their whole agenda is to promote abortion rights," said a staff member of the National Conference of Catholic Bishops Diocesan Development Program for Natural Family Planning. The same staff member who attended the mid-April preparatory sessions at U.N. headquarters in New York, said a press conference cosponsored by Catholics for a Free Choice and Planned Parenthood included speakers who referred to the Holy See as "basically a religious terrorism group" which in their view supports "extremism and fundamentalism that's destructive to people's lives."

A letter from pro-abortion women's groups distributed to delegates attending the International Conference on World Population and Development specifically attacked the Catholic Church, including a charge that "the Vatican claims to defend life while at the same time opposing measures to save women's lives, including modern contraception, condoms, safe abortion and women's rights." The letter also charged that the Vatican "ignores the daily tragedy of 400 deaths due to unsafe abortion." The statement stated further that "to impose one religious perspective on a whole continent or worldwide is imperious and unacceptable."

The president of Catholics for a Free Choice, spoke at the April press conference, saying the Vatican opposed "enlightened access to family planning, to sterilization and to abortion." I remember only too well that in the 1930s an "enlightened leader" also endorsed family planning, sterilization, and abortion. His name was Adolph Hitler.

As a result of the Pope's highly visible stand against abortion speaking directly to Conference participants, as well as opposition to the plan from Muslim countries, the pro- abortion forces failed to reach consensus in Cairo. Shamelessly, U.S. officials had promised huge money grants to complying nations.

For years division has been developing within the American Catholic Church between those loyal to the Vatican and those opposed. I feel it may be only a short time before this division surfaces and possibly splits the American Catholic Church. What a tragedy it would be if that time ever comes. Prayer and conversion as requested by our Blessed Mother can prevent this from happening.

APPARITIONS. At Fatima, in 1917, our Blessed Mother told three young children,

> Say the Rosary every day to obtain peace for the world... I come to ask the consecration of Russia to My Immaculate Heart and the communion of reparation on the first Saturdays. If they listen to my requests Russia will be converted and there will be peace. If not she will scatter her errors through the world, provoking wars and persecutions of the Church. The good will be martyrized, the Holy Father will suffer much, various nations will be annihilated.

When the apparitions started in Medjugorje in 1981, the messages of our Blessed Mother repeated the requests She made at Fatima. This time, however, the messages of Mary were unique in the history of the Church in regards to their detail and frequency (daily apparitions since 1981).

In October 1981, our Blessed Mother told the visionaries in Medjugorje the following:

1. Regarding Poland,

> There will be great conflicts, but in the end, the just will take over.

2. Regarding Russia and the West,

> The Russian people will be the people who will glorify God the most. The West has made civilization progress, but without God, as if they were their own creators.

In 1987 I worked as a staff specialist in the office of the Assistant Secretary of Defense for Communications and Intelligence. My responsibility included development of electronic self-protection and intelligence collection systems for aircraft and ships. All our planning was to provide for complex systems capable of operating effectively against the Warsaw Pact nations if a conflict took place in Central Germany. Our plans took us beyond the year 2000. If, in 1987, I could have been able to predict the events of 1989 to 1991 in Eastern Europe and told everyone exactly what eventually took place, what do you think the government would have done to me? Nobody in 1987, not the Pentagon, the CIA, the great "know it all" media, could have foreseen events that were about to unfold in Eastern Europe — the fall of communism and the reunification of Germany within a two-year period without a shot being fired.

Now everyone has answers why communism in Eastern Europe collapsed so fast! Conservatives tell us it resulted from our military build-up under President Reagan plus the Russian economy, which could not keep up the arms race. But our own economy lagged also. And I wonder how long we would have lasted with ever increasing budget deficits. Liberals tell us communism fell because of misery, hunger, poverty, and oppression. However, it was not too long ago that many liberals said life under communism was not so bad in the Soviet Union and was what the Russian people preferred. Conservatives and Liberals use these excuses because they cannot comprehend where the credit truly belongs. Maybe they do not want to contemplate that it could have been miraculous intervention by God. In 1991 my cousin's husband received a letter from his brother in Israel who belonged to an extreme ultra-orthodox Jewish sect. In the letter he stated events occurring in Eastern Europe (i.e., fall of communism and split up of the Soviet Union) are a result of the messiah having come and the redemption of the Jewish people and all mankind would soon be at hand. That a Jew saw in these events God's hand at work, that He has finally sent the messiah to bring redemption, amazed me. Many Christians have difficulty seeing God's hand in all of this. Even some Fatima devotees wonder if the fall of the Soviet Union was related to the promise Mary told Sister Lucia.

In addition to reported apparitions in Medjugorje, there have also been an unprecedented number throughout the world during the last 15 years with messages by our Blessed Mother similar to those given in Medjugorje. Local bishops approved several apparitions, but many still are under investigation. Many are probably false. After all, even Satan can do apparently "nice" things to mislead people.

PREPARATION FOR CHRIST'S COMING

If our Lord is indeed coming soon, who better than Mary can prepare us for that event? She calls us back to holiness much in the same way as ancient prophets continually called the people of Israel back to God to prepare them for our Lord's first coming. How blest we are. Mary, Who respects our free will, asks us lovingly to accept Her messages freely. If we live the messages, which are really the Gospel of our Lord, we need not fear the future. Unfortunately, too many concentrate only on prophetic "impending" disasters and tribulations prior to our Lord's return. This is wrong. We should be relentless in bringing God's love and mercy to those in need, using His miraculous tools: the Sacraments, especially the Eucharist, the Holy Spirit, and Mary our Mother. He bestows this power upon us, if we pray, especially the Rosary, to effectively change and bring about conversions. While there is still time, we must use all our energy to bring Christ's love and forgiveness, not condemnation, to a world living as if God does not exist. We should pray for enlightenment for those Catholics criticizing our Holy Father who do not follow his or the Church's teachings. Our Lord gave this commission to all Christians before His ascension and it still remains in effect. Put all our trust in Him; we will be amazed what we can accomplish as His instruments.

At this critical time, the Church needs once again to emphasize Jesus Christ crucified, especially through its preaching, in the manner of Saints Peter and Paul. When I first entered the Church in 1963 I heard many "fire and brimstone" sermons. I honestly did not care for this type of preaching and still do not. The Apostle Paul spent his entire Christian life preaching Christ crucified to the Gentiles. Why do we seem to have such a problem talking about Jesus' suffering and death? Does it conjure up our guilt? The passion and death of our Lord is the greatest act of love, compassion, humility, and forgiveness the world has ever known or will know. Jesus experienced this agony because of His unconditional love for us. We did not earn it or even deserve it.

Most Protestant churches display crosses but not crucifixes. Protestants will tell you Jesus was resurrected and lives in Heaven; therefore, there is no need for a crucifix depicting His suffering and death. Today some Catholic Churches revere the figure of Jesus on the Cross dressed as Christ the King (i.e., with a beautiful robe and crown). Messianic Jews, who try to bring other Jews to believe in Jesus as the Messiah, have no crosses. They say that the Cross to Jews is a sign of persecution of Jews by Christians. How sad.

Mary tells us in Medjugorje:

Dear children, renew prayer before the Cross. Dear children, I am giving you special graces and Jesus is giving you special gifts from the Cross. Take them and live! Reflect on Jesus' Passion and in your life be united with Jesus! (February 20, 1986)

Jesus, by means of His Cross, leads us through our own exodus. We are still in the world, suffer, and must face death. Looking at and praying before a crucifix makes our exodus durable. I believe that

125

Jesus rose from the dead and is now glorified at the right hand of the Father. But while I still live in this world, it is His passion and death with which I can best identify. When bad things happened to me I usually went to Church, knelt before a crucifix, and realized that my sufferings were nothing compared to His suffering and death. Since my conversion, I have never looked at suffering as a sign of God's rejection. I know He loves each of us and His love is unconditional. Two of Mary's messages come to mind:

> I desire that your cross also would be a joy for you. Especially, dear children, pray that you may be able to accept sickness and suffering with love the way Jesus accepted them. Only that way shall I be able with joy to give out to you the graces and healing which Jesus is permitting me. (September 11,1986)

> Dear children, you will be able to receive Divine love, only in proportion to when you understand that, on the Cross God offers you His immense love. (February 22,1986)

Many years ago I attended a mission during lent at a local parish. The priest gave a beautiful talk about Jesus on the Cross. Essentially, he said that whenever you have difficulties or experience a loss or pain, go and kneel before a crucifix. Then ask Jesus if He loves you. Listen and you will hear in your heart His words, "What more can I do for you?" And if you still are not sure go to God the Father and ask Him if He loves you. You will hear the Father say, "Look at the Cross. That is my Son, the only Son I ever had. What more can I do for you?" If I may add, we could ask Mary the same question as we look at Her holding in Her arms the dead body of Her only Son after He is taken down from the Cross.

St. Peter and Paul saw the glorified Christ. Yet because they preached Him crucified, they, along with other Apostles and disciples, assisted by the Holy Spirit, ensured the rise of Christianity. They gave their lives for our Savior. Can we do less? When our Lord returns, it will please Him if He finds us living and spreading the Gospel with great joy and hope, rather than hanging around waiting and watching for great tribulations many of which have already occurred, are still occurring today, and will yet occur. It is good to recall Jesus' own words regarding the true disciple:

> It is not those who say to me, 'Lord, Lord', who will enter the kingdom of heaven, but the person who does the will of my Father in heaven. When the day comes many will say to me, 'Lord,

Lord, did we not prophesy in your name, cast out demons in your name, work many miracles in your name?' Then I shall tell them to their faces: I have never known you; away from me, you evil men! Therefore, everyone who listens to these words of mine and acts on them will be like a sensible man who built his house on rock. Rain came down, floods rose, gales blew and hurled themselves against that house, and it did not fall; it was founded on rock. But everyone who listens to these words of mine and does not act on them will be like a stupid man who built his house on sand. Rain came down, floods rose, gales blew and struck that house, and it fell; and what a fall it had! (Matthew 7:Zl-27)

CHAPTER 12
MARY, THE MOTHER OF GOD

After having spent half my life as a Jew, before becoming Catholic, it is my humble opinion that if Christians had a better understanding of ancient Jewish tradition and truly knew our Lord and God Jesus Christ, they would see the importance of Mary in salvation history. They would come to realize that the tribute and honor Catholic and Orthodox churches have accorded Her throughout the centuries do not even begin to do Her justice.

All Bible-reading Christians recognize the great people mentioned in the Scriptures: Abraham, Moses, Isaiah, John the Baptist, Peter, and Paul. But how much do they know about Mary, the Mother of Jesus, the singularly most wonderful person ever created. She is unique for two special reasons.

Reason One: God chose to redeem the world by being born of a woman. Yet His coming into the world and our redemption depended on Mary freely saying:

I am the handmaid of the Lord, let what you have said be done to me. (Luke 1:38)

This young Jewish woman, like all Her people, anxiously awaited the Messiah. Once again it is important to recall that no Jew thought the Messiah would be God in the form of man and be born of a virgin. Jews, including Mary and Joseph, did not identify the prophecy in Isaiah 7:14 with the birth of the Messiah. Only after the Holy Spirit came on Her did Mary probably first understand the following prophecy cited by St. Matthew:

Now all this took place to fulfill the words spoken by the Lord through the prophet: the virgin shall conceive and give birth to a son and they will call Him Immanuel, a name which means 'God-is-with-us.' (Matthew 1:22-23)

Mary, although full of grace, could not have fully comprehended at the time Her future destiny. Yet She unconditionally trusted in God and totally committed Herself to His will.

Reason two: It was from Mary that our Lord Jesus took His flesh and blood since He had no human father. To whom was it ever said:

Of all women You are the most blessed, and blessed is the fruit of Your womb. (Luke 1 :4Z)

Chapter 8, the last chapter of the most important document issued by Vatican Council II, entitled, "The Blessed Virgin, Mother of God, in the Mystery of Christ and the Church," states in the introductory passage:

The Virgin Mary who at the message of the angel received the Word of God in her heart and in her body and gave life to the world, is acknowledged and honored as being truly the mother of God and mother of the redeemer. Redeemed in a more sublime manner by reason of the merits of her Son and united to him by a close and indissoluble tie, she is endowed with the high office and dignity of being the mother of the Son of God, by which account she is also the beloved daughter of the Father and the temple of the Holy Spirit. Because of this gift of sublime grace she far surpasses all creatures, both in heaven and on earth. At the same time, however, because she belongs to the offspring of Adam she is one with all those who are to be saved. She is 'the mother of the members of Christ... having cooperated by charity that faithful might be born in the Church, who are members of that head'. Wherefore she is hailed as a preeminent and singular member of the Church, and as its type and excellent exemplar in faith and charity. The Catholic Church, taught by the Holy Spirit, honors her with filial affection and piety as a most beloved mother. (53)

If Orthodox Jews could be convinced that Jesus Christ was truly their awaited Messiah and also God, their understanding of Mary's role and their devotion to Her, would probably surprise most Christians. Most Jewish converts to Catholicism have a great devotion to our Blessed Mother. I have never heard or seen our Blessed Mother, yet I doubt that the visionaries to whom She appears have an understanding of Mary, which I have been graced with, because of my Jewish background.

In chapter 4, I discussed the innermost sanctuary in the original Temple of Jerusalem called the Holy of Holies, the abode of Yahweh, which housed His throne, the Ark of the Covenant. The Ark held the two stone tablets on which God wrote the Ten Commandments. No one, except the High Priest could enter the Holy of Holies, and then only once a year on the Day of Atonement. Recall that the belief of Yahweh's presence in His Temple was the sole reason for worship being celebrated there and for pious customs of the faithful. No one could touch the Ark of the Covenant and live. In the second book of Samuel we read:

> **Uzzah walked alongside the ark of God and Ahio went in front. David and all the House of Israel danced before Yahweh with all their might singing to the accompaniment of lyres, harps, tambourines, castanets, and cymbals. When they came to the threshing-floor of Nacon, Uzzah stretched his hand out to the ark of God and steadied it, as the oxen were making it tilt. Then the anger of Yahweh blazed out against Uzzah, and for this crime God struck him down on the spot, and he died there beside the ark of God.** (2 Samuel 6:4-8)

Our Blessed Mother is greater than the Holy of Holies in the original temple.

> **The Word was made flesh and He lived among us and we saw His glory, the glory that is His as the only Son of the Father, full of grace and truth.** (John 1:14)

In the Holy of Holies God's presence appeared in the form of a cloud. In Mary's womb our Creator and God was conceived and lived. In all creation, then, is there anything more sacred than Mary? The womb of Mary is more sacred than the Holy of Holies. The Holy of Holies contained the sacred Ark of the Covenant. But in Mary's womb resided the Covenant Maker. She is therefore the True Ark.

After destruction of the Temple by Romans in 71 A.D., Jewish worship centered around the Torah in the synagogue. Recall that I discussed the Torah in chapter 2. The Torah is the most sacred object for Jews. I remember, when as a teenager attending Sabbath morning services in the synagogue, the reverence everyone expressed for the Torah. When the Torah was taken out of its receptacle, known as the Ark, it would be displayed by ceremonial procession around the synagogue before being placed on a table for the reading of the appropriate part for that day. While the Torah was processed men and boys would go over to it and kiss it. I will never forget an eighty year-old blind man who every week would be led over to the Torah so that he could embrace and kiss it. When I saw the look on his face I imagined the look on Moses' face after he first encountered God in the fire on Mt. Horeb. The Torah is only a scroll which contains the written word of God. Within the womb of Mary was the Word Itself, our Lord and God.

For me, there is nothing created by God more holy or sacred than our Blessed Mother. And the real beauty is that each person can touch Her, feel Her, experience Her. We do not have to be the Pope to have Her for support. We can be assured She is always there to help us. If we would only listen and live Her messages then we would realize She constantly intercedes for us with God.

I have a tough time understanding why Mary is almost entirely ignored by most Protestants and many Catholics. In fact, some are uneasy about the position Mary holds in Catholic teaching, even ignoring Her because it might have an adverse effect on Christian unity. I find words inadequate to describe what true devotion all who call themselves Christian owe to the Blessed Virgin Mary.

My comments regarding Mary stem from my Jewish background. Even if the Church said nothing about Mary, I would still honor Her above all other creation as long as I acknowledged Jesus as my God and Savior. But the Church has said a lot about Mary throughout the centuries. The Church has pronounced dogmas concerning Mary and given Her many titles. It is on a few of these dogmas and titles I would like to comment briefly.

Scripture contains only brief commentaries about Mary. Most of our devotion and understanding of Her comes from Church tradition. There is a good reason for this. The New Testament writings essentially cover a period of about 40 years, dealing mostly with the three-year ministry of Jesus and the early Church until the deaths of Peter and Paul in Rome around 68 A.D. During those years Jesus first had to convince His apostles and disciples that His messiahship was not what they had been expecting: that is, the Messiah was God become man, had to suffer and die, and that He was not going to restore the kingdom to Israel immediately. Considering the immense task of the early Church to make Jesus and His Gospel known, the New Testament writings are extremely limited. It was John who wrote:

There were many other things that Jesus did; if all were written down, the world itself, I suppose, would not hold all the books that would have to be written. (John 21:25)

Paul, in his first letter to the Corinthians, tells us the difficulty he encountered.

> And so while Jews demand miracles and the Greeks look for wisdom, here are we preaching a crucified Christ, to Jews an obstacle that they cannot get over, to pagans madness... (I Corinthians 1:22-24)

The focus then in this early church and during the formation of the New Testament writings rightly belonged on Jesus and not Mary. It was not until 431 A.D., that the Church Council of Ephesus, finally declared Jesus as being True God and True Man. What we believe about Mary must always be looked at in relation to Her Son and God's plan of salvation for us. In this way the Church's teachings concerning Mary never cause conflict with Sacred Scripture. They even draw their strength from them because God the Holy Spirit Who inspired the Scriptures also directs Tradition.

IMMACULATE CONCEPTION

In Chapter 8 of the Constitution in the Church, Vatican Council II, we read the following:

> Adorned from the first instant of her conception with the radiance of an entirely unique holiness, the virgin of Nazareth is greeted, on God's command, by an angel messenger as 'full of grace' (Luke 1:28), and to the heavenly messenger she replies: 'Behold the handmaid of the Lord, be it done unto me according to thy word': (Luke I:38.) Thus Mary, a daughter of Adam, consenting to the divine Word, became the mother of Jesus. Embracing God's salvific will with a full heart and impeded by no sin, she devoted herself totally as a handmaid of the Lord to the person and work of her Son, under him and with him, by the grace of almighty God, serving the mystery of redemption. (56)

In the East, the Church celebrated the Feast of the Immaculate Conception as early as the seventh century. For the Greeks, initiators of the feast, the expression "Immaculate Conception" meant that Mary, from the first moment of Her life, was preserved from sin. Did it also mean that she was spared even original sin? Latin theology stands firm on two things: (a) every human being is infected with original sin and bears its consequences; (b) this hereditary sin is remitted through the merits of Christ, Redeemer of the entire human race.

Pope Pius IX, on December 8,1854, proclaimed Mary preserved from original sin, beginning with the moment of her conception. The privilege accorded Her stems from the source and basis of Mary's essential impeccability, acknowledged since the first centuries of Christianity. Said the Pope:

We declare, proclaim, and define that this dogma is revealed by God and therefore to be firmly and unremittingly believed by all the faithful: namely the dogma which holds that the most slessed Virgin Mary, from the first moment of her conception, by a singular grace and privilege from Almighty God and in view of the merits of Jesus Christ was kept free of every stain of original sin.

Three things may be noted in this definition:

(1) The nature of Mary's privilege. It is, properly speaking, an immunization. Original sin is depicted as a sort of contagion that affects all human beings (except the God- Man, Jesus) and "soils" them. From this comes the attraction to evil residing in each of us. Nothing of the sort was found in Mary, who did not experience the disorder introduced by the first parent, Adam, into his descendants.

(2) The ground of the privilege. The definition takes account only of the singular grace accorded to Mary "in view of the merits of Christ." But Tradition, much cited in considerations of the privilege, finds reason for this singular grace in the Divine plan that destined Mary to become the Mother of God and could not tolerate her being, even for an instant, in the power of the devil.

(3) The mode of preservation. It was by a "preventive" effect of the Redemption gained on Calvary that Mary was preserved from original sin. Jesus is Redeemer of all human beings, and there is no sanctifying grace imaginable apart from His one, universal act of Redemption. This law applies also to Mary, even though She received the grace "in view of the merits of Her Son," i.e., before the fact, and not subsequent to it as with the rest of us.

From February 11 to July 18,1858, our Blessed Mother appeared eighteen times to a 14 year old girl named Bernadette Soubirous in the French city of Lourdes. On March 25,1858, Feast of the Annunciation, the Lady revealed Her name: **"I am the Immaculate Conception"**. Today this great shrine approved by the Church claims about 4 million visitors each year who come seeking spiritual and physical cures. They also come to pray for conversions and to honor our Lord and His Mother.

EVER VIRGIN

Most Christians accept that Mary conceived our Lord as a virgin. Matthew writes:

> **This is how Jesus Christ came to be born. His mother Mary was betrothed to Joseph; but before they came to live together she was found to be with child through the Holy Spirit.** (Matthew 1:18)

The question for many is whether Mary remained a virgin all Her life. In calling Mary "ever virgin" Catholic Tradition is saying that after conceiving Jesus in virginity Mary always remained a virgin, abstaining from all conjugal relations. This also implies that the birth of Jesus left intact the virginity of His Mother.

Most Protestants and many Catholics do not believe Mary remained a virgin after Jesus' birth and they usually cite Scripture for their reasons. The Catholic Church contends, however, that the Gospels furnish no argument against the teaching that Mary was "ever virgin." Once again my Jewish background helps me see clearly the Church's position, expressed in the following four points.

1. Jesus is called first-born, implying for many Christians that Mary had other children. If a Jewish child is a boy and the first in the family, another ceremony follows a month after the birth. It is called Pidyon Haben, which literally means "to redeem the first-born male." According to biblical injunction, every firstborn male of the womb whether man or animal is considered as belonging especially to the Lord (Exodus 13:1-2). The bible commanded human beings were to be redeemed and clean animals sacrificed (Leviticus 27:26). In olden times the redemption consisted in the payment of five shekels, or their equivalent, to be made to a priest thirty days after the birth of the first son. Redemption was always considered the release from Temple service. This could mean acting as priests, musicians, or servants in Jerusalem. The practice proved a hardship on many families; naturally the parents did not want to part with their older children. Eventually the tribe of Levi was set aside to serve in the Temple in place of the firstborn. A passage in the book of Numbers reads:

> **And I behold have taken the Levites instead of every firstborn; and the Levites shall be mine.** (Numbers 3:12-13; 45-51)

In accordance with this relaxation of the original laws every firstborn male child has to be redeemed. This means he is freed from service at the Temple by the payment of five shekels to a Levite who serves in his stead. Since Jesus was from the tribe of Judah, He had to go through the rite of redemption. St. Luke describes this rite, performed when Mary and Joseph presented Jesus in the Temple. (Luke 2:22-24). I went through this rite 30 days after my birth since I was the first-born. I was an only child. Yet I was still called firstborn.

2 . On several occasions the Gospels speak of "brothers of Jesus, "for example, James and Joseph (Matthew 13:55). But these are sons of another Mary, expressly named "the mother of James and Joseph" (Matthew 2 7 :5 6) who cannot be identified with the Mother of Jesus and who also is always named after Mary Magdalene. Besides, in the Semitic world the name brothers often applies to relatives and confederates. Abraham says to his nephew Lot: **"We are brothers"** (Genesis 13:8).

3. Matthew declares:

Joseph had no relations with [Mary] at any time before she bore a son, Jesus. (1:25)

The Semitic locution before... or until... makes no judgement about the future. Thus:

Michal was childless until the day of her death. (2 Samuel 6:23)

4. The episode of the Finding in the Temple and especially the episode on Calvary where Jesus entrusts His Mother to a disciple (John 19:25-27) seem to imply that Mary had no other children. But in any case, the very ancient Tradition of Mary's perpetual virginity was never historically questioned at a time when the memory of "brothers of Jesus" remained part of the vernacular.

The incident that most convinces me Mary and Joseph continued to live in chastity after the birth of Jesus was the Annunciation. When the Angel Gabriel appeared to Mary and announced that She was to conceive a Son, who would be called the Son of the Most High, She responded,

But how can this come about, since I am a Virgin? (Luke 1:34)

Mary was betrothed to Joseph at the time. According to ancient custom, Jewish tradition includes two stages to matrimony. First comes betrothal and then marriage. Betrothal, the ceremony by which a woman becomes engaged to the man who betroths her, binds her (from her side), in a union that culminates in marriage. She is forbidden to marry anyone else, unless her betrothed dies or divorces her. Why did Mary deem it necessary to remind Gabriel that She was a virgin? If Mary and Joseph had intended to live a normal married life according to Jewish custom, then Gabriel's annunciation to Her should have meant simply that after Her marriage She would conceive naturally (i.e., Joseph would be the natural father). The child could still be called "Son of the Most High" because no one, not even Mary and Joseph, expected the Messiah to be God. Mary's question to Gabriel only makes sense to me if Mary and Joseph had consecrated their lives to God and had intended to live chaste lives even after their marriage, because Mary intended to remain a virgin all of Her life. I know this is hard for us to understand, in this sexually enlightened age, that a married couple could be so dedicated to God they would live together in chastity.

Yet once Mary and Joseph realized, with the help of the Holy Spirit, that Her Son was indeed God and for nine months would grow in Her womb, how could they even contemplate having other children? Mary was now greater than the Old Temple, Her womb,too, now greater than the Holy of Holies. How could anyone else enter or live in the womb where Jesus our Lord resided before His birth? One writer sums this up beautifully as follows:

"Mary and Joseph, after the miraculous conception, their motive was to put themselves entirely and exclusively at the service of Jesus, and to renounce everything that might conceivably divert or distract them from playing their full part in His mission. Their motive was not lack of esteem for the married life (unthinkable in Judaism) or even the prizing of continence as a higher ideal than the consummation of marriage. Their choice was motivated exclusively by the fact of the virginal conception, by the desire to serve this child. The virginal conception was both an invitation and a call, to Her who was to be the Mother of the Lord. What possible response could Mary have made except that of exclusive dedication to the work of Him who is mighty, Who had done such great things for Her?... Certainly, it is not so much because of Her physical virginity as because She gave Jesus the undivided love of Her soul that the Church extols Her as Virgin most venerable, Virgin most renowned, Virgin most faithful. Mary continued 'as She was when the Lord called her' and She always kept Her virginity to 'devote Herself entirely to the Lord.' (1 Corinthians 7:17- 35)."

The belief in Mary's perpetual virginity already appears wide-spread by the second century. Many of the early Church Fathers, such as Origen (died 254), Saints Ambrose, Jerome, and Augustine, strongly defended the virginity of Mary, before and after the birth of Jesus. Many Catholics are surprised to learn that leading Protestant reformers of the sixteenth century — Luther, Zwingli, and Calvin among them — asserted and preached Mary's perpetual virginity.

ASSUMPTION OF MARY

By the authority of our Lord Jesus Christ, of the Blessed Apostles Peter and Paul, and by our own proper authority we pronounce, declare, and define as Divinely revealed dogma that Mary, Immaculate Mother of God ever Virgin, after finishing the course of Her life on earth, was taken up in body and soul to heavenly glory.

By these words Pope Pius XII, exercising Pontifical Infallibility, "declared" on November 1, 1950, that the Assumption was a dogma of faith and was henceforth to be believed as such by the faithful (Bull Munificentissimus).

The language of the Definition expresses its object precisely: "having finished the course of her life on earth," Mary was "glorified in body and soul." That is to say, Mary is already in the state that will be true of the elect after the "resurrection of the dead." This implies a transition from the bodily state proper to life on earth to the mysterious but real state, proper to eternal life.

In the case of Mary, how did the transition occur? Was it by an immediate transformation without going through death, i.e, without prior separation of the soul from the body? Or was it by an anticipated resurrection, which presupposes that Mary was dead? The definition purposely does not take a position on this point. It remains a question that theologians may freely debate. Discussion aside, let it simply be said that the opinion that Mary, like Her Son, passed through death in order to be raised up, immediately or after a short interval, has by far the stronger support in tradition.

In no way did the question of a new revelation arise. Hence, if the Assumption was to be declared a "Divinely revealed dogma," it had to be contained in the established sources of Revelation. The Bull Munificentissimus takes note of this, saying that the "ultimate basis" of the defined truth was found in Sacred Scripture. However, in referring it to the Bible the papal document does not mean to suggest that the Assumption can be "read" there in an immediate and explicit manner. In the present state of biblical scholarship, it seems difficult to go beyond this statement: that the dogma of the Assumption, "Divinely revealed," is really contained in Revelation in an implicit manner.

The Feast of the Assumption of Mary is one of the oldest and most solemn feasts of the Church. Its history dates back to at least the seventh century when the feast day was already celebrated at Jerusalem and Rome.

What is the Meaning of the Assumption of Mary? A culmination! **"Blest is she who trusted..., who believed"** (Luke 1:45). The promises of the Lord were fulfilled for Mary, and as always, beyond all expectation. Her glorification in body and soul results from Divine love. But it also came, so to speak, as the logical conclusion of Her vocation on earth and the way She lived it. She lived Her Divine Motherhood in utter harmony with Her Assumption, the same as with Her Immaculate Conception and perpetual virginity, both called for by the supernatural motherhood. How could the body of Her in whom **"the Word was made flesh"** to save the flesh have known the corruption of the grave? Or the body of Her who totally escaped the power of sin? And the body of Her Who, by Her virginal consecration, belonged to Her Son and His mission in a perfect and exclusive way?

If anyone has followed Christ to the utmost, without the least failing, it is Mary. How, then, could He not gather Her with Him, body and soul, to the glory which the Cross represents as the way and the door? What other reward could be imagined for Mary than this immediate and total participation in the life of the Risen Lord? Some day all the blessed will rise at the resurrection and together with our Mother Mary, totally participate in the life of Christ.

MOTHER OF GOD

The title "Mother of God" is not found as such in the writings of the New Testament. Yet Elizabeth, Mary's cousin, calls Mary the Mother of my Lord.

Yahweh, the name of God in Hebrew, is usually translated LORD in most English Bibles except for the Jerusalem Bible, which maintains the Hebrew word. Jews never pronounced this divine name. It was used only once a year on the feast of Atonement or Yom Kippur, when the high priest entered the Holy of Holies in the Temple in Jerusalem (Leviticus 16). In the worship services in orthodox synagogues, *Adonai* or **"Our Lord"** substitutes for Yahweh. One prayer that Jews recite during the daily and Sabbath services in the synagogue can be recognized by Catholics as the beginning of the Sanctus.

Holy, Holy, Holy is the Lord of hosts; the whole earth is full of your glory.

The last prayer a Jew should recite before death is called the great *Shema.*

Hear O Israel, the Lord our God, the Lord is One. (Deuteronomy 6:4)

After Her conception Mary goes to visit and assist Her cousin Elizabeth who is six months pregnant. St. Luke in his Gospel gives us a vivid account of the arrival at Elizabeth's house (Luke 1:39-58).

Now as soon as Elizabeth heard Mary's greeting, the child leapt in her womb and Elizabeth was filled with the Holy Spirit. She gave a loud cry and said, 'Of all women you are the most blessed, and blessed is the fruit of your womb. Why should I be honored with a visit from the mother of my Lord.' (Luke 1:41-43)

When a Jew uses the word Lord, she or he refers to God. Elizabeth, a Jew filled with the Holy Spirit, realizes that the Child in Mary's womb is not just some human messiah but her Lord (God). In a sense we can say that Elizabeth was the first person to acknowledge our Blessed Mother Mary as the Mother of God.

The first known mention of the title Mother of God comes from St. Hippolytus of Rome (died 235 A.D.). The Council of Ephesus (431 A.D.) condemned Nestorianism which denied the unity of the divine and human natures in the Person of Christ. It also defined Theotokos (Bearer of God) as the title of Mary, Mother of the Son of God made Man. The Church explicitly promulgated as dogma the decision made at Ephesus in 451 A.D. by the Council of Chalcedon. Vatican Council II states in Chapter 8 on the Constitution on the Church:

The reality of the Divine Motherhood explains the human and supernatural perfection of Mary. It is the only case in which a 'Son' was able to 'fashion' His Mother as He wanted her to be. This Son is all-powerful. He could not but prepare for Himself a Mother worthy of Him, a 'worthy Mother of God,' totally devoted to her exceptional vocation: 'Redeemed by reason of the merits

of her Son and united to Him by a close and indissoluble tie, she is endowed with the high office and dignity of being the Mother of the Son of God and, in consequence, the beloved daughter of the Father and the temple of the Holy Spirit. Because of this sublime grace she far surpasses all creatures, both in heaven and earth. (LG 53)

MEDIATRIX

A "Mediator" is one who stands between two persons or groups of persons either to facilitate an exchange of favors or, more often, to reconcile parties at variance. As applied to Mary, the title "Mediatrix" dates back to the sixth century in the East and to the ninth century in the West. Since the seventeenth century, Mediatrix has been widely used by Catholics everywhere.

Our Lady may be styled "Mediatrix" under one of three conditions. (1) As worthy Mother of God and full of grace, she occupies a "middle" position between God and His creatures. (2) Together with Christ and under Him, She cooperated in the reconciliation of God and humankind while She was still on earth. (3) She distributes the graces which God bestows on His children. In whichever of these three meanings it may be taken, Mary's mediation must always be understood as being secondary to, and dependent on, Christ's primary and self-sufficient mediatorial role.

When we say that our Lady is Mediatrix as dispenser of graces, we mean that all favors and blessings granted by God to His rational creatures are granted in virtue of and because of Her intervention. The manner in which She exercises Her role is, specifically, by way of intercession. It is not necessary that we explicitly implore Her intercession in our prayers. But whether we mention Her or not, it is through Her that we receive whatever we receive. Since She is our loving Mother in the supernatural realm, She knows our needs and wishes to help us in all of them; and since She is the Mother of God, Her prayer on our behalf cannot but be most powerful and efficacious.

The Council Fathers at Vatican Council II state in Chapter 8 on the Constitution:

There is but one mediator as we know from the words of the apostle, 'for there is one God and one mediator of God and men, the man Christ Jesus, who gave himself a redemption for all' (I Tim, 2, 5-6). The maternal duty of Mary toward men in no way obscures or diminishes this unique mediation of Christ, but rather shows his power. For all the salvific influence of the blessed virgin on men originates not from some inner necessity, but from divine pleasure and from the superabundance of the merits of Christ. It rests on his mediation, depends entirely on it and draws all its power from it. In no way does it impede, but rather does it foster the immediate union of the faithful with Christ. (LG 61)

This maternity of Mary in the economy of grace began with the consent she gave in faith at the annunciation and sustained without wavering beneath the cross; it lasts until the eternal fulfillment of all the elect. Taken up to heaven she did not lay aside this salvific duty, but by her constant intercession continued to bring us the gifts of eternal salvation. By her maternal charity, she cares for the brethren of her Son, who still journey on earth surrounded by dangers and difficulties, until they are led into the happiness of their true home. Therefore the blessed virgin is invoked by the Church under the titles of advocate, auxiliatrix, adjutrix, and mediatrix. This, however, is to be so understood that neither takes away from, nor adds anything to, the dignity and efficaciousness of Christ the one mediator. For no creatures could ever be counted as equal with the incarnate Word and redeemer. (LG 62)

During my life as a Jew, Mary meant nothing to me. Only when I realized that Jesus was my God, did I know then that Mary was also my Mother. And I thank Jesus for sharing His Mother with me. By honoring Mary, I honor Jesus Her Son. Many times in the past I have gone and will continue to go to Mary and ask Her for help by praying or speaking to Her Son for me. Just as I would ask any Christian to pray for me to Jesus. Mary's place and honor were not given Her by the Church. They were given Her by God the Father in choosing Her, by the Holy Spirit in overcoming Her, and by Her Son in being born of Her. Mary can never be an obstacle to Jesus. She can only lead us to Her Son.

Since Vatican Council II, we have preached a lot about love, talked a lot about love, but for the most part we fail to live it. That is why we have abortion, child abuse, divorce, drug addiction, the homeless, world starvation, and racism. I stated earlier that in this life we come closer to God through love than through knowledge. We know this from the Scriptures, especially New Testament writings. It is much easier to have or gain knowledge than to love and be vulnerable. We all, clergy, religious and laity, need to come closer to our Mother Mary. We need to imitate Her. Mary's virtues, i.e., Her love, Her obedience, Her patience, Her suffering, must also become our virtues. Then Jesus will live in us and shine through us, as He lives and shines through His Mother Mary.

TWICE CHOSEN

CONCLUSION

As a Jew, I was taught about the God of Abraham, Isaac, Jacob, Moses, and the Prophets. In accepting Jesus as my Lord and Savior I have not abandoned Judaism. It is only in Jesus Christ that I can see the Father Who is God of all people and desires their salvation.

I can find no better way to end this book than with Mary's great hymn of praise, the Magnificat, and St. Paul telling us we must be the same as Christ in his letter to the Philippians.

We read in Luke's Gospel, chapter 1:46-55:

And Mary said:
'My soul proclaims the greatness of the Lord, [1 Sm 2:1]
My spirit exults in God My Savior; [Is 61:10]
because He has looked upon His lowly handmaid. [1 Sm 1:11; Ps 113:7; Zeph 3:12]
Yes, from this day forward all generations will call Me blessed, for the Almighty has done great things for Me [Ps 71:19; 126:2f]
Holy is His name [Ps 111:9]
His mercy reaches from age to age for those who fear Him. [Ex 20:6; Ps 85:9; 103:17]
He has shown the power of His arm, [Ps 98:1; Is 40:10]
He has routed the proud heart. [Jb 5:12; Ps 33:10;138:6]
He has pulled down princes from their thrones and exalted the lowly. [Jb 5:11; Ps 75:8]
The hungry He has filled with good things, [Ex 34:29]
the rich He sent empty away. [1 Sm 2:5; Ps 34:10f; 107:9]
He has come to the help of Israel His servant, [Is 41:9] **mindful of His mercy —** [Ps 98:3; Jer 31:3, 20]
according to the promise He made to our ancestors — of His mercy to Abraham and to his descendants for ever [Gn 13:15; 22:18; Ps 132:11]

Mary's song of praise brings together the major themse of Old Testament piety as shown by the references given next to the text. The Magnificat totally infuses the faith and hope of Israel. For Christians, the importance of the Magnificat is found most of all in the event which Mary celebrated: the conception of Jesus. This is by far the most striking and most decisive of the great things that God has done for the salvation of His people. It is also the reason why Christian generations have made the Magnificat the favored expression of their own experience of salvation in Jesus Christ. The movement of soul that called forth Mary's song of thanksgiving is in fact the same sort of inward movement that emerges in the faith of the Christian. In Mary's case, the actual experience of God's presence served to illuminate Her future as well as Her past.

Mary leads all of Her children to Her Son Jesus. She essentially tells us that our attitude must be like Her Son's. St. Paul in his letter to the Philippians (2:1-11) describes that attitude:

> In the name of the encouragement you owe me in Christ, in the name of the solace that love can give, of fellowship in spirit, compassion, and pity, I beg you: make my joy complete by your unanimity, possessing the one love, united in spirit and ideals. Never act out of rivalry or conceit; rather, let all parties think humbly of others as superior to themselves, each of you looking to the others' interests rather than to his own. Your attitude must be that of Christ: Though He was in the form of God, Jesus did not deem equality with God something to be grasped at. Rather, He emptied Himself and took the form of a slave, being born in the likeness of men. He was known to be of human estate, and it was thus that He humbled Himself, obediently accepting death, death on a cross! Because of this, God highly exalted Him and bestowed on Him the name above every other name. So that at Jesus' name every knee must bend in the heavens, on the earth, and under the earth, and every tongue proclaim to the Glory of God the Father: JESUS CHRIST IS LORD!

Having been undeservedly blessed by God, I can now pray:

"HEAR, O ISRAEL THE LORD OUR GOD, THE LORD IS ONE: FATHER, SON, AND HOLY SPIRIT."

MAY GOD BE PRAISED!

REFERENCES

Catholic Book Publishing Co., Dictionary of Mary, New York, 1985.

De Montfort, St. Louis, The Secret of the Rosary, TAN Books and Publishers, Inc., Rockford, IL, 1988.

De Montfort, St. Louis, True Devotion to the Blessed Virgin, Montford Publications, Bayshore, NY, 1987.

Deiss, Lucien, God's Word and God's People, The Liturgical Press, Collegeville, MN, 1974.

deVaux, O.P., Roland, Ancient Israel, McGraw Hill Book Co., Inc., New York, 1961.

Doubleday & Company, Inc., The Jerusalem Bible, New York, 1968.

Goldin, Judah, The Living Talmud, New America Library of World Literature, Inc., New York, 1964.

Goldstein, David, What Say You, Radio Replies Press, Minnesota, 1945.

Hardon, S.J., John A., American Judaism, Loyola University Press, 1971.

Heinisch, Paul, Theology of the Old Testament, The Liturgical Press, Collegeville, MN, 1955.

Marian Helpers Center, Devotion to the Divine Mercy, ~1993 Congregation of Marians, Stockbridge, Massachusetts; printed with permission; all world rights reserved.

Michalenko, C.M.G.T., Sr. S., Mercy My Mission, Marian Press, Massachusetts, 1987.

Minkin, Jacob S., The World of Moses Maimonides, New York, 1957.

Miravalle, Dr. Mark, Heart of the Message of Medjugorje, Franciscan University Press, Steubenville, OH, 1988.

Our Sunday Visitor Publishing Division, Catholic Almanac, Indiana, 1990.

Paulist Press, The Constitution on the Church of Vatican Council II, Deus Books, New Jersey, 1965.

Plastaras, C.M., James, The God of Exodus, The Bruce Publishing Co., Milwaukee, 1966.

St. James Publishing, Words From Heaven, Two Friends of Medjugorje, Birmingham, Al., 1990.

The Catholic University of America, The New Catholic Encyclopedia, Washington, D.C., 1966.

United States Catholic Conference, Inc., Catechism of the Catholic Church, English Translation, Washington, D.C., 1994.

United States Catholic Conference, Rich in Mercy, Encyclical, November 30,1980, 1981.